The 9/11 Investigation

by Craig E. Blohm

LUCENT BOOKS
A part of Gale, Cengage Learning

GALE
CENGAGE Learning™

Detroit • New York • San Francisco • New Haven, Conn • Waterville, Maine • London

LIBRARY OF CONGRESS CATALOGING-IN-PUBLICATION DATA

Blohm, Craig E., 1948-
  The 9/11 investigation / by Craig E. Blohm.
     p. cm. -- (Crime scene investigations)
  Includes bibliographical references and index.
  ISBN 978-1-4205-0136-0 (hardcover)
  1. September 11 Terrorist Attacks, 2001--Juvenile literature.
  2. Terrorism--United States--Juvenile literature. I. Title. II. Title: Nine-eleven investigation.
    HV6432.7.B55 2009
    364.152'34097471--dc22

                                              2009021314

32.00

Lucent Books
27500 Drake Rd.
Farmington Hills, MI 48331

ISBN-13: 978-1-4205-0136-0
ISBN-10: 1-4205-0136-4

Printed in the United States of America
1 2 3 4 5 6 7 13 12 11 10 09

Contents

Foreword

The popularity of crime scene and investigative crime shows on television has come as a surprise to many who work in the field. The main surprise is the concept that crime scene analysts are the true crime solvers, when in truth, it takes dozens of people, doing many different jobs, to solve a crime. Often, the crime scene analyst's contribution is a small one. One Minnesota forensic scientist says that the public "has gotten the wrong idea. Because I work in a lab similar to the ones on *CSI*, people seem to think I'm solving crimes left and right—just me and my microscope. They don't believe me when I tell them that it's the investigators that are solving crimes, not me."

Crime scene analysts do have an important role to play, however. Science has rapidly added a whole new dimension to gathering and assessing evidence. Modern crime labs can match a hair of a murder suspect to one found on a murder victim, for example, or recover a latent fingerprint from a threatening letter, or use a powerful microscope to match tool marks made during the wiring of an explosive device to a tool in a suspect's possession.

Probably the most exciting of the forensic scientist's tools is DNA analysis. DNA can be found in just one drop of blood, a dribble of saliva on a toothbrush, or even the residue from a fingerprint. Some DNA analysis techniques enable scientists to tell with certainty, for example, whether a drop of blood on a suspect's shirt is that of a murder victim.

While these exciting techniques are now an essential part of many investigations, they cannot solve crimes alone. "DNA doesn't come with a name and address on it," says the Minnesota forensic scientist. "It's great if you have someone in custody to match the sample to, but otherwise, it doesn't help.

That's the investigator's job. We can have all the great DNA evidence in the world, and without a suspect, it will just sit on the shelf. We've all seen cases with very little forensic evidence get solved by the resourcefulness of a detective."

While forensic specialists get the most media attention today, the work of detectives still forms the core of most criminal investigations. Their job, in many ways, has changed little over the years. Most cases are still solved through the persistence and determination of a criminal detective whose work may be anything but glamorous. Many cases require routine, even mind-numbing tasks. After the July 2005 bombings in London, for example, police officers sat in front of video players watching thousands of hours of closed-circuit television tape from security cameras throughout the city, and as a result were able to get the first images of the bombers.

The Lucent Books Crime Scene Investigations series explores the variety of ways crimes are solved. Titles cover particular crimes such as murder, specific cases such as the killing of three civil rights workers in Mississippi, or the role specialists such as medical examiners play in solving crimes. Each title in the series demonstrates the ways a crime may be solved, from the various applications of forensic science and technology to the reasoning of investigators. Sidebars examine both the limits and possibilities of the new technologies and present crime statistics, career information, and step-by-step explanations of scientific and legal processes.

The Crime Scene Investigations series strives to be both informative and realistic about how members of law enforcement—criminal investigators, forensic scientists, and others—solve crimes, for it is essential that student researchers understand that crime solving is rarely quick or easy. Many factors—from a detective's dogged pursuit of one tenuous lead to a suspect's careless mistakes to sheer luck to complex calculations computed in the lab—are all part of crime solving today.

A Weapon of Terror

At 6:38 P.M. on December 21, 1988, Pan American World Airways Flight 103 took off from London's Heathrow Airport, beginning a routine transatlantic journey that was scheduled to end in New York City. The aircraft, a Boeing 747 bearing the fanciful name *Clipper Maid of the Seas*, carried 243 passengers and a crew of 16. No one on board could have known that the plane would never reach its destination. At 7:06 P.M. the jumbo jet was flying high over the Scottish countryside when a tremendous explosion ripped through the aircraft. Within seconds tons of debris, burning fuel, and human remains were raining down on the small town of Lockerbie. "It was like meteors falling from the sky,"[1] commented one resident. Eleven people on the ground were killed, as were all on board the aircraft. Of the 243 passengers on the *Clipper Maid of the Seas* that fateful night, 189 were Americans.

Why did Pan Am Flight 103 explode? While it could have been a catastrophic mechanical failure, something more sinister—a bomb—was also possible. It was up to forensic investigators to find out, and their task would not be easy. Wreckage from the crash was spread out over hundreds of square miles on the ground. Search crews collected thousands of pieces of debris, some just tiny fragments of metal, plastic, or cloth. One of those fragments was a piece of an electronic circuit board no larger than a fingernail. Investigators determined that it was part of a timing device often used by terrorists to detonate bombs. Further investigation led to the arrest of two Libyan men, one of whom was eventually convicted of the bombing.

Explosives have long been a weapon of choice for hate groups and terrorists, who want to inflict the most amount of

*The explosion of
Pan Am Flight 103
in 1988 destroyed
houses and left
a deep gash in
the ground near
Lockerbie, Scotland.*

damage on their targets. By their nature, the massive destruction that explosives cause makes it extremely difficult to determine the type, origin, and ultimately the maker of the device. Without a claim of responsibility by a person or group, forensic science is one of the best tools available to determine the facts of a case. Armed with extensive knowledge, sophisticated scientific equipment, and dogged determination, forensic investigators can extract vital clues from minute traces left at a crime scene after a blast. Often these clues mean the difference between solving a difficult crime and relegating it to the "cold case" file.

Explosives are used not only for their destructive power, but also for their ability to "send a message" to those whom their creators consider their enemies. On September 15, 1963, a bomb exploded in the Sixteenth Street Baptist Church, an African American church in racially divided Birmingham, Alabama. Four young girls lost their lives in the blast, and the church was heavily damaged. Although physical evidence was scarce, it was not difficult to determine why the church was bombed. Birmingham was a center of the emerging civil rights movement in the early 1960s, a movement that many Southern whites opposed. The Sixteenth Street Church attack was the deadliest of many bombings carried out in Birmingham to strike fear in the hearts of African Americans in their struggle for equality. It was a tragic example of domestic terrorism in America.

International terrorists also use explosives to broadcast their message to the world. They select high-profile targets such as military bases and commercial buildings to obtain the maximum propaganda effect. In 1983 a suicide bomber crashed an explosive-laden truck into the lobby of a U.S. Marines barracks in Beirut, Lebanon. When the bomber detonated the explosives, the building collapsed, killing 241 American military personnel. In 1993 another truck bomb detonated at the Twin Towers of the World Trade Center in New York City. The terrorists' plan was to destroy the foundation of the north tower, sending it toppling into the south tower to destroy both in a single, massive attack. Although one tower was damaged, both remained standing. Just two days after the blast, with the crime scene still dangerously unstable, federal and local investigators combed the basement of the north World Trade Center tower where the truck had been parked. Among the rubble were parts of the truck that had survived the blast. On one piece investigators found an identifying number that led them eventually to identify the terrorists involved in the plot, including the one who drove the deadly truck into the World Trade Center.

PI/1353

PI/1232

PI/911

PI/1806

PK/2075

PK/1310A

PI/1808 PI/1807 PI/1803

PI/1388 PI/1420 PI/1431 PI/1466 PI/1487 PI/1488 PI/1538

PI/1545 PI/1548 PI/1552 PI/1564 PI/1565 PI/1589 PI/1590 PI/1591

PT/22

PI/1643 PI/1644 PT/24 PT/25 PT/68

PT/23

CMS 10 20

PP8932

Pieces of the suitcase that contained the bomb that exploded on Flight 103 are shown here. Many different everyday objects can conceal bombs.

Explosive devices do not always look like deadly weapons; they can take on the most innocent of forms. The explosives that brought down Flight 103 were concealed in an inexpensive cassette tape player placed aboard the plane in an ordinary suitcase. Mailboxes, parcels, and soda cans are all everyday objects that can conceal bombs. Vehicles of all types can also be used to hide explosive devices. Automobiles are perfect for such attacks, as they are seen everywhere but rarely given a second glance. In the 1993 attack on the World Trade Center, the terrorists converted a common rental truck into a rolling bomb to carry out their plan. Investigators determined that if the explosives had been a bit larger or the truck parked at a different spot, the plan could have succeeded. Eight years later, terrorists would use another type of vehicle to deliver a blow to the World Trade Center. Commercial airliners would be the vehicles, their fully loaded fuel tanks containing all the explosive power the terrorists could want. And unlike in 1993, this time the terrorists would succeed.

CHAPTER ONE

Terror from the Skies

September 11, 2001, dawned much like any other morning in New York City. It was a Tuesday, with a brilliant blue sky and balmy temperatures heralding what promised to be a beautiful early fall day. New York is one of the busiest cities in the world, and by eight o'clock people were bustling along the streets, heading to work in the countless office buildings that form the distinctive skyline of Manhattan Island. Manhattan is a major financial and cultural center of the United States and one of the leading centers of commerce in the world. It is home to the influential New York Stock Exchange and the headquarters of countless business and financial industries. Many of these corporate offices were located in the towers of the World Trade Center. Situated in the lower Manhattan financial district, the World Trade Center was a complex of seven buildings, the most prominent of which were twin aluminum-clad office towers rising 110 stories above the ground.

To people around the world, New York City is a symbol of America's wealth and financial power. For some, that symbol is a beacon of the seemingly endless opportunities that are available in the United States. For others, however, it has become a symbol of American arrogance; cultural prejudice; and a relentless, imperialistic quest for world domination.

Flight 11

About 190 miles (306km) northeast of New York City, at Boston's Logan International Airport, American Airlines Flight 11 pushed away from the gate and rolled toward the taxiway. The Boeing 767 had a capacity of 158 passengers, but today the cabin was only about half full, with 81

This American Airlines Boeing 767 is similar to Flight 11 that left Boston with 81 passengers and 11 crew members.

passengers and a crew of 11 on board for an early morning flight to Los Angeles. Among the crew was flight attendant Betty Ong, who was traveling to Los Angeles on the first leg of a planned vacation to Hawaii. The passengers on Flight 11 were a cross-section of ordinary Americans, from secretaries and engineers to college students and businessmen. No one paid much attention to five Middle Eastern–looking men seated throughout the cabin.

At 7:59 A.M. Flight 11 lumbered down the runway and climbed into the clear morning sky. Since this was to be a transcontinental journey, the plane's fuel tanks were fully loaded with 76,400 pounds (34,654kg) of highly combustible aviation fuel. This much fuel was needed for the 2,600-mile (4,184km) trip to the West Coast. But if it fell into the wrong hands, American Flight 11 could become a flying bomb.

Airborne Weapons

In the space of forty-five minutes after Flight 11 took off, three other aircraft also began their flights. At 8:14 A.M. United

Airlines Flight 175 departed from Boston's Logan Airport, carrying sixty-five passengers and crew on their way to Los Angeles. Six minutes later, American Airlines Flight 77 took off from Washington, D.C.'s Dulles International Airport, also heading for Los Angeles. On board were sixty-four passengers and crew. After experiencing delays of almost forty-five minutes, United Airlines Flight 93 finally roared down the runway of Newark International Airport (now Newark Liberty International Airport) in New Jersey. The aircraft turned west, heading for San Francisco with its load of forty-four passengers and crew. These three flights all had similarities to American Flight 11. They were jumbo jets carrying less than their full complement of passengers. Each one was scheduled to make a cross-country flight, and thus was loaded with highly volatile jet fuel.

And in the cabin of each aircraft sat a group of hijackers waiting for the right moment to take over the plane and turn it into a missile of destruction.

By the Numbers

1,000

Number of first responders called to the World Trade Center.

Terror in the Sky

The first indication that something out of the ordinary was happening on Flight 11 came as air traffic controllers were routinely monitoring the flight from the air traffic control center outside of Boston. Shortly after 8:14 A.M. the controller monitoring Flight 11 radioed the pilot instructions to climb to 35,000 feet (10.7km). Pilots routinely confirm that they have heard such a message, but no reply came from Flight 11. "American 11, this is Boston Center, how do you read?"[2] a controller repeated, but still no one answered. Then controllers noticed something strange on the radar display. All commercial aircraft have a device called a transponder that transmits information such as flight number, altitude, and heading to the ground. Although the bright blip representing the plane

The terrorists on Flight 11 said they were returning to the airport but instead headed toward the World Trade Center in Manhattan.

was still visible, vital information about Flight 11 was not displayed. Someone had turned off the transponder.

In the plane, flight attendant Betty Ong picked up an air-to-ground telephone and called an American Airlines office in North Carolina. "The cockpit is not answering, somebody's stabbed in business class—and I think there's Mace—that we can't breathe—I don't know, I think we're getting hijacked."[3]

Although Ong was in the rear of the plane and could not see what was taking place in the cockpit, she was correct: Flight 11 had been taken over. Earlier that morning five men boarded the Boeing 767, passing through Logan Airport's security with no difficulty. Once Flight 11 had reached cruising altitude, the terrorists made their move. Brandishing knives, they stabbed two flight attendants and a passenger. The terrorists then broke into the cockpit, overpowering the pilots and taking control of the airplane.

On the ground, controllers heard an ominous radio transmission from Flight 11. "We have some planes. Just be quiet and stay calm. We're returning to the airport."[4] The voice had a distinct accent; one of the hijackers was trying to calm the passengers. But he had pushed the wrong button, and instead of talking on the cabin's public address system, he was transmitting his message to the ground. Seconds later another transmission came from the plane. "Nobody move. Everything will be okay. If you try to make any moves, you'll endanger yourself and the airplane. Just stay quiet."[5] It confirmed to the controllers that the aircraft was now in the hands of terrorists.

Three More Planes

Aboard the other three flights—United Flights 175 and 93 and American Flight 77—a similar scenario was playing out. On each flight, a group of terrorists broke into the cockpit and took control of the aircraft. Passengers using cell phones reported horrifying scenes on board the aircraft. "It's getting bad, dad," passenger Peter Hanson on United 175 said in a call to his father. "A stewardess was stabbed . . . the plane is making jerky movements . . . I don't think the pilot is flying the plane."[6]

All of the hijacked aircraft began flying erratically, losing altitude and deviating from their original flight plans. Air traffic controllers listened for further radio transmissions and continued trying to contact the flights. Controllers also began directing other air traffic to stay clear of the commandeered planes. American Flight 11, originally headed for Los Angeles, turned south on a new course, taking the plane in the general direction of New York City. United 175 altered its course, also heading toward New York. American Flight 77, which had originated in Washington, D.C., flew all the way to Ohio, then made a sharp turn and doubled back toward the nation's capital.

United Flight 93 had been routinely following its flight plan for the first forty-five minutes of its trip. Then, at 9:27 A.M., controllers in Cleveland, Ohio, heard what seemed to be sounds of a fight being transmitted from the aircraft. They heard the international distress call, "Mayday," and then a voice shouting, "Hey, get out of here!"[7] This confirmed that Flight 93 had also been hijacked. Forced to the back of the cabin by the hijackers, several passengers used seat-back telephones or their cell phones to call friends or family members. Through these calls, passengers learned of the other three hijacked planes.

Target: World Trade Center

At 8:41 A.M., about the time United Flight 93 was taking off, air traffic controllers were following Flight 11's erratic progress toward New York City. The terrorists had said that they were returning to the airport, and controllers thought they might be headed for New York's Kennedy Airport. In the cockpit of Flight 11, hijacker Muhammad Atta sat behind the controls. He was indeed flying the plane toward New York, but his destination was not the airport. Like her colleague Betty Ong, flight attendant Amy Sweeney was in the back of the plane on the phone. "Something is wrong," she said. "We are in a rapid descent . . . we are all over the place." A few seconds later, Sweeney cried, "We are flying way too low. . . . Oh my God we are way too low."[8] Then, silence.

On a street corner about 1 mile (1.6km) from the World Trade Center, two French filmmakers, brothers Gédeon and Jules Naudet, were shooting a scene of a documentary video about New York City firefighters. As the camera captured firefighters checking for a gas leak on the street, the microphone picked up the sound of an airplane overhead. Jules, who was operating the camera, panned it up from the street scene to the skyline where the Twin Towers of the World Trade Center stood gleaming in the early morning sun. Suddenly a cloud of smoke and fire erupted from the north tower of the World Trade Center as American Airlines Flight 11 crashed into the building at nearly 500 miles per hour (805km/h). It was 8:46 A.M., forty-seven minutes after the aircraft took off.

The Second Tower

The terrorists aboard United Flight 175 took over the plane at about the same time that Flight 11 smashed into the World Trade Center's north tower. Upon breaking into the cockpit, they seized the controls and turned the plane onto a course toward New York. Herded to the back of the aircraft, passengers made phone calls to family and acquaintances on the ground. Some already realized that their situation was grave. Peter Hanson, still on the phone with his father, said, "I think we are going down—I think they intend to . . . fly into a building."[9]

United Flight 175 hit the south tower of the World Trade Center at 9:03 A.M.

Shortly after Flight 11 hit the World Trade Center, television networks suspended their regular programming and began broadcasting live video of the scene. Viewers around the country were shocked to see a huge plume of smoke pouring from high up in the north tower (also called 1 World Trade Center). Reporters did not know what kind of plane it was or why it had hit the building. Speculation ran from a private pilot making a disastrous navigation error to a plane flying out of control due to a mechanical malfunction.

In the New York television studio of ABC's *Good Morning America*, host Charles Gibson was talking to a reporter who was on the scene in lower Manhattan. As Gibson watched a live shot of the World Trade Center on a monitor, the south

Eyewitness to Terror

One of the most distinctive aspects of the collapse of the World Trade Center is the unprecedented media coverage of the disaster. Newspaper reporters, still photographers, television camera crews, and radio correspondents spent the morning of September 11, 2001, recording and reporting incredible sights and sounds. Often the reporters themselves were caught up in the disaster. Anne Thompson, an NBC news correspondent, found herself in the dust cloud of the collapsed south tower:

> I was at 195 Broadway, a commercial office building about a block and a half from the Trade Center. I turned my back to the cloud, wedged myself between a column and the wall, and covered my face. For five minutes, it just seemed to rain down this ash of destruction.
>
> I initially tried to hold my breath. But the rain of ash went on for so long that at one point I had to breathe. I exhaled, and then I inhaled, which was a huge mistake, because the air was so thick. I started to choke. I tried not to breathe through the rest of it.

Quoted in Allison Gilbert, Phil Hirschkorn, Melinda Murphy, Robyn Walensky, and Mitchell Stephens, eds., Covering Catastrophe: Broadcast Journalists Report September 11. *Chicago: Bonus, 2002, pp. 82–83.*

tower (2 World Trade Center) suddenly erupted in smoke and flame. "That looks like a second plane has just hit . . . ," Gibson exclaimed. "The second explosion, you could see the plane come in just from the right-hand side of the screen, so this looks like some concerted effort to attack the World Trade Center that is underway in downtown New York."[10]

United Flight 175, with the hijackers at the controls, hit the south tower of the World Trade Center at 9:03 A.M.

Target: Pentagon

By now it was obvious that the United States was under attack by an as yet unknown enemy. The two tallest buildings in New York City were on fire, and police and fire officials were organizing a massive rescue operation. The fact that the attacks occurred early in the morning meant that many offices might be empty, awaiting the first arrivals of the day. Some 200 miles (322km) away, in Arlington, Virginia, another office building was also beginning its work day. But rather than being a monument to America's commercial strength, this building was home to the nation's military establishment.

The Pentagon, named for its five-sided shape, was built in 1942 out of a need for a single military headquarters as the

The Pentagon took a direct, devastating hit from Flight 77, which crashed into the building at an estimated 530 miles per hour.

United States entered World War II. By 2001 some twenty-three thousand military and civilian people worked in the Pentagon's 3.7 million square feet (343,741 sq. m) of office space. About twenty thousand people were at their desks on the morning of September 11.

Hijacked Flight 77 was flying back toward Washington, D.C., where it had originated. As with the other flights, the armed hijackers forced the passengers to the rear of the cabin. As the aircraft approached the nation's capital, air traffic controllers feared that the plane would be flown into one of Washington's many government buildings. Controllers at Ronald Reagan Airport informed the Secret Service that "an aircraft [is] coming at you and not talking with us."[11] Flight 77 began losing altitude over Virginia, until, at about 9:34 A.M., it was flying at 2,000 feet (610m) about 4 miles (6.4km) from the Pentagon. Then the hijacker at the controls pushed the throttles to maximum power as the plane screamed toward the Pentagon.

An Arlington County police officer, patrolling several miles away from the Pentagon, saw the low-flying airplane and moments later observed a plume of smoke rising in the direction the plane had been headed. The officer grabbed his radio microphone: "We just had an airplane crash . . . must be in the District area."[12] Flight 77 had crashed into the west wall of the Pentagon at an estimated 530 miles per hour (853km/h).

A Mission Thwarted

Three airliners hijacked—three buildings hit. That left one more plane in the hands of terrorists, ready to attack another unsuspecting target. But the passengers aboard United Flight 93 were not about to let that happen without a fight.

By the Numbers

17,000

Approximate number of people in the Twin Towers on 9/11.

Huddling in the back of the cabin, several passengers formulated a plan: They voted to rush the cockpit and try to wrest control of the plane away from the hijackers. Passenger Tom Burnett told his wife, Deena, on the phone, "We can't wait. Deena, if they are going to run this plane into the ground, we're

"Let's Roll!"

In the tragic story of the 9/11 attacks, no group of people is more heroic than the passengers of United Airlines Flight 93. And no two words are more remembered than those spoken by Todd Beamer, a passenger on that doomed flight.

Todd Beamer was a thirty-two-year-old account manager for a software company when he boarded Flight 93 on September 11, 2001. After the plane was commandeered, Beamer and other passengers moved to the rear of the plane. Learning through phone calls that three other hijacked planes had been used as flying bombs, Beamer and several other men decided that they would try to prevent that from happening to Flight 93. The men, all strong, athletic types, agreed to assault the cockpit and try to take control from the hijackers. As the moment arrived, Beamer turned to his colleagues. "Are you ready? Okay. Let's roll!"

It is not known for sure if the men made it into the cockpit. But their daring attempt convinced the terrorists that the hijacking would not succeed. Flight 93 plunged to the earth in Pennsylvania, far from its intended target in Washington, D.C.

"Let's roll" became a rallying cry for America in the war on terrorism. An emblem with an eagle, an American flag, and the words *Let's Roll* was painted on aircraft flying missions in Afghanistan.

Quoted in Lisa Beamer with Ken Abraham, Let's Roll! *Wheaton, IL: Tyndale House, 2002, p. 217.*

going to do something."[13] Todd Beamer, on the phone with Lisa Jefferson, a phone company supervisor, explained their plan to her. "Are you sure that's what you want to do, Todd?"[14] she asked. "It's what we have to do,"[15] Beamer replied.

For the next several minutes the cockpit voice recorder taped the sounds of the struggle for control of Flight 93. Screams and crashes were heard, as well as the hijackers arguing among themselves. Finally, chilling words came from the cockpit. "Pull it down! Pull it down!"[16] said one of the hijackers as the pilot pushed the wheel hard right, rolling the plane onto its back.

In an empty field in the Pennsylvania countryside, the tranquil morning of September 11, 2001, was shattered by the sound of screaming jet engines and a thundering crash. At 10:03 A.M. United Flight 93 slammed into the ground at 580 miles per hour (933km/h), blasting a crater 50 feet (15m) deep and completely disintegrating the Boeing 757. Although the flight ended in tragedy, a greater tragedy was averted. For it is almost certain that the hijackers had intended to crash the aircraft into either the White House or the U.S. Capitol. The brave passengers of Flight 93 had thwarted the armed hijackers and died as heroes.

Wounded Buildings

Flight 11 had hit 1 World Trade Center between the ninety-third and ninety-ninth floors, creating a jagged gash spewing dense, dark smoke that enveloped the entire top of the building. Sirens screamed as police cars, fire engines, ambulances, and rescue vehicles raced through the streets of lower Manhattan toward the towers. By 9:00 A.M., just fourteen minutes after the crash, hundreds of firefighters from all over the city were already on the scene. Pedestrians walking to work just moments before were now panicked by the horrifying scene. College student Kimberly Morales later recalled: "I was terrified. I stood there on the sidewalk for about two minutes. Everything around me was going crazy. People were running everywhere and screaming about two planes."[17]

Like its twin to the north, the south tower, 2 World Trade Center, was belching smoke and fire from the hole torn into the building by Flight 175. The plane had hit the tower between the seventy-seventh and eighty-fifth floors. The billowing plume of smoke from the towers was being blown southward by the wind, creating a dark smudge over the New York skyline that was visible for miles. The planes had hit the towers so high that no ladders were tall enough to reach the burning floors. Firefighting and rescue efforts would have to be carried out from inside the buildings. Burdened with air

The billowing smoke from the towers could be seen for miles.

tanks, hoses, axes, and other heavy gear, firefighters began to make their way up the stairs in the World Trade Center. As they headed up they encountered people fleeing down from the floors below the damaged areas of the buildings. John Labriola, who worked on the seventy-first floor of the north tower, recalled his escape:

> Around the 35th floor, we started meeting the stream of firefighters walking up. None of them said a word. I can't stop thinking about the look in their eyes, how heroic they were. . . . We had to press into a single file so the firefighters could march past. They were carrying unbelievable loads of equipment, and were already exhausted by the time we started seeing them.[18]

Labriola was one of the lucky ones; he made it safely out of the World Trade Center, along with almost everyone below the impact zone. For those above the burning floors, however, the story was grim. With elevators out of operation, doors warped shut, and stairwells clogged with fire and debris, there was little chance of escape. Some tried to escape to the roof, only to find the doors locked. In any case, the heat and smoke billowing up from the towers would have made a rooftop rescue by helicopter impossible. And time was running out.

"It's Inevitable"

At 9:59 A.M. the south tower of the World Trade Center collapsed, engulfed in a roiling cloud of smoke and dust. So much debris filled the air that it obscured what had happened. NBC's Matt Lauer told his television audience, "I don't know whether it's another explosion or a portion of the building falling away, but something major just happened to that building."[19] As the smoke gradually lessened, the truth was revealed: 2 World Trade Center was gone. The force of its collapse spread dust and debris for blocks around the World Trade Center. People covered their mouths and ran to escape the approaching cloud of thick, choking dust.

High overhead, officers in police helicopters had a clear view of the destruction below. Through the pall of smoke they could see the north tower still burning furiously. "I don't think this has too much longer to go," radioed police chopper pilot Greg Semendinger. "I would evacuate all the people in the vicinity of the second building."[20] Another pilot, Tim Hayes, agreed: "About fifteen floors down from the top, it looks like

People cover their faces as they rush away from the thick dust caused by the towers collapsing.

its glowing red. It's inevitable."[21] Unfortunately, the people trapped in the tower and the firefighters who came to help them could not know how close the inevitable was. At 10:28 A.M. the north tower stood alone, abandoned by its fallen twin. Then, the north tower slowly fell in on itself, an end almost identical to the collapse of the south tower.

Becoming a Forensic Pathologist

Job Description:
A forensic pathologist is a medical doctor who specializes in determining causes of death by performing autopsies and examining soft tissue samples. Forensic pathologists will often be called to testify in court.

Education:
A forensic pathologist must have a doctor of medicine (MD) degree, with additional training in pathology. A three- to five-year residency in pathology after receiving the MD degree is usually required.

Qualifications:
A forensic pathologist must be comfortable working in a laboratory as well as at a crime scene, often in unpleasant circumstances. He or she must have keen powers of observation, an inquisitive mind, and the ability to create written reports and present oral testimony in court.

Additional Information:
Certification by the American Board of Pathologists is recommended.

Salary:
Approximately $80,000 to over $200,000 per year.

The destruction of the World Trade Center left behind more than just dust and rubble. It left behind the remains of innocent civilians and heroic rescue workers. It left behind devastated families, some frantically trying to learn if loved ones had survived, others mourning those they knew were lost. It left behind an America shocked and wounded. But most of all, the 9/11 attacks left behind questions: How could such a thing happen in the United States? Were more attacks on their way? Can we as a nation ever feel safe again? Answers would come in due course, but the first order of business was to find and identify the victims and then find and identify the people responsible for the attacks. For these jobs, the work of forensic investigators would prove crucial in the weeks and months after 9/11.

CHAPTER TWO

The Search at Ground Zero

In August 1945 the world's first atomic bomb exploded over Hiroshima, Japan, ultimately leading to the surrender of Japan and the end of World War II. The point on the ground directly beneath the explosion was known as Ground Zero. For decades after the war, the phrase "ground zero" was best known as a military term used to describe the point of maximum damage of an explosion. Until September 11, 2001.

After the collapse of the World Trade Center, the area where the 110-story towers had stood became known as Ground Zero for its landscape of utter devastation. Journalists at the scene had a difficult time describing the enormity of the disaster. Peter DeMarco, a reporter for the *New York Daily News*, wrote:

> The size of Ground Zero was at first overwhelming. The towers' 220 stories seemingly had been run through a gigantic office shredder, reduced to mountains of concrete slivers, tangled wires, steel pipes, rebar, office chairs, computer monitors, papers, and other bits and clumps. Like a cauldron, the mass smoldered in places, and though it was midday, the fallen debris had pockets as dark as caves.[22]

No one knew if there were any survivors trapped in the rubble. But it was certain that there were many victims of the tragedy entombed below the jagged concrete and twisted steel. It would be a massive job to locate and identify these victims and bring closure to their families.

The utter devastation where the World Trade Center and nearby buildings were destroyed became known as Ground Zero.

Rescue or Recovery?

A search-and-rescue mission is one in which survivors of an accident or disaster are searched for and brought to safety. In a search-and-recovery mission, it is assumed that there are no survivors, and all effort is aimed at retrieving bodies. Despite the devastation at Ground Zero, there was still the possibility

29

With the extent of the damage, rescue efforts soon gave way to recovery efforts at Ground Zero.

that some people had survived the collapse and now lay buried under tons of rubble. Thousands of police officers, firefighters, construction workers, and volunteers began the search for survivors in the enormous pile of wreckage. They looked below the pile for voids, areas clear of debris where someone may have been trapped after surviving the collapse. It was extremely hazardous work, as the rubble was unstable and fires beneath the wreckage still burned at temperatures often exceeding 1,800°F (982°C). At the outset, rescue workers removed the debris with their bare hands, concerned that using bulldozers and other heavy equipment might further the collapse, killing anyone buried below.

Few people were rescued. Only twenty survivors were found alive under the rubble at Ground Zero, the last person rescued some twenty-seven hours after the World Trade Center collapsed. For weeks rescuers continued to look for survivors. Using shovels and buckets they removed tons of debris from the pile in a valiant but ultimately futile effort to find more survivors. New York mayor Rudolph Giuliani announced, "We don't have a substantial amount of hope to offer to people that there is anyone alive in there."[23] On September 29, the mission officially changed from search and rescue to search and recovery. One of the many problems with the recovery effort soon became clear: No one knew how many victims there were.

Numbers

As one of the largest office complexes in the United States, the World Trade Center was normally filled with people. Office workers, government employees, building maintenance people, security guards, restaurant and shop staff, and visitors all made up the diverse population of the towers. On a typical weekday some forty thousand to fifty thousand people came to work in the Twin Towers. Thousands more visited the buildings to attend business meetings, have lunch, or marvel at the view of Manhattan from the observation deck on the 107th floor of the south tower. It was fortunate that the attacks came before the population of the towers had reached its peak. Still, there was a considerable number of people at the World Trade Center on the morning of September 11, and no one knew exactly how many.

"It quickly became clear to us," wrote Shiya Ribowsky of New York's Office of the Chief Medical Examiner (OCME), "from what we knew of the Trade Center's population during

By the Numbers

19,858

Number of body parts recovered from Ground Zero.

Recovering the Remains

The process of recovering the remains took place in several steps. While excavation was taking place at Ground Zero, on-site "spotters" would call a halt to backhoe operations if suspected remains were seen. Just before the debris left the site, it was given a second look to locate remains. The debris was then transported to the specially designated landfill, where examiners on either side of a conveyor belt examined the debris for personal effects and any potential remains.

Once an official sample was identified at any of these locations, it was transported to the morgue, where a forensic anthropologist from the medical examiner's office would determine whether the sample was actually human. Because of several restaurants in the complex, there were samples of chicken and hot dogs initially identified as human remains. If determined to be human, a sample then went to the temporary morgue set up by the disaster mortuary response team.

a business day, that the death toll would be far in excess of anything we had ever expected. . . . [There were] initial estimates of up to 30,000 fatalities." Whenever a violent or suspicious death occurs in New York City, the medical examiner's office is notified. Its job is to investigate and determine the cause of death, issue death certificates, provide forensic information to be used in court, and identify the deceased in cases where the identity is missing or unclear. Ribowsky was a medicolegal investigator—a forensic scientist often referred to as a crime scene investigator. As the OCME's director of identifications, Ribowsky was responsible for establishing a system to identify the victims of the 9/11 attacks. It was, as Ribowsky put it, "a task of monumental proportions: processing and identifying the remains of those thousands who did die. Not only was the scale of the disaster unique, but it set for us a series of logistical challenges that would change forever the way the OCME conducted its business—and the way New York City counted its dead."[24]

Two Types of Disasters

Forensic investigators classify disasters that result in a massive loss of life into two broad categories. Closed population disasters, such as airplane crashes, have an identifiable group of victims. Closed disasters are easier to investigate, because

Workers look through debris from the World Trade Center at the Fresh Kills facility on Staten Island. Mayor Giuliani designated the landfill site as the receiving point for World Trade Center debris.

victims can usually be identified by such documents as passenger lists and records of ticket purchases. In open population disasters, the victims are unknown. Earthquakes or commuter train crashes, for example, are considered open disasters. Open disasters present a far more difficult situation because both the number of casualties and their identities are unknown. In such cases other means must be used for victim identification.

The 9/11 attacks presented investigators with a situation that combined both open and closed disasters. The victims on the airplanes, the closed population, could be identified through passenger manifests acquired from the airlines, a relatively simple task. The people in the towers, however, made up the open population of the 9/11 disaster. Who had been in the buildings when the towers collapsed? Forensics was the only way to find out.

By Wednesday, September 12, disaster crews were already removing large amounts of rubble from Ground Zero. There was soon so much broken concrete and steel that a place had

Managing a Disaster Scene

1 Rescue living victims and provide first aid as needed.

2 Prioritize the injured by severity of injuries (triage).

3 Assure the scene is safe for rescue workers to enter.

4 Secure the scene to prevent unauthorized entry.

5 Preserve all items of potential evidence.

6 Locate witnesses and take statements.

7 Forensically investigate the scene.

to be found to put it all. Mayor Giuliani designated a landfill site on nearby Staten Island as the receiving point for World Trade Center debris. Somewhat unfortunately called Fresh Kills (the name actually comes from the Dutch and means "freshwater stream"), the facility began receiving barge loads of rubble from Ground Zero. New York Police Department and Federal Bureau of Investigation (FBI) teams sorted through the rubble, looking for the remains of victims, as well as any evidence that might lead to identifying the terrorists. Fresh Kills, like Ground Zero, was now an official crime scene.

Triage

At the OCME an incident command center was set up to organize the tasks of receiving and examining the remains. To store bodies and body parts prior to examination, refrigerated trucks were set up outside the OCME; they would be the first stop for incoming remains. The morgue was divided into areas where the various forensic tasks would take place: fingerprinting, DNA collection, X-rays, dental examination, and other operations necessary for identifying the deceased.

Because of the total devastation of the World Trade Center, a majority of the remains coming into the OCME were only fragments of human beings. Bones, either large pieces or small fragments, were often the only evidence remaining of a person that had been in the towers. But it was often difficult to determine if a recovered fragment was a human bone, an animal bone (there were restaurants and food shops in the towers), or simply a piece of concrete, which could resemble a shard of bone. In addition, many bone fragments were embedded in other material due to the force of the tower collapse. So triage became the first step in the identifications process. *Triage*, from a word that means "sift," is used in hospitals to determine the order of treatment in hospital emergency rooms. Patients who are severely injured or very ill receive treatment before those cases that are less serious. In the OCME a forensic anthropologist performed triage to determine the authenticity of human bone fragments.

Amy Mundorff, a forensic anthropologist at the OCME, worked with the triage team as body bags of remains came in. She recalls: "Each bag was examined to eliminate unassociated and unattached parts within a body bag. Every piece of human remains that was not attached to another by hard or soft tissue was segregated."[25] Mundorff continues: "Every fragment of bone and tissue was removed and placed in its own bag for individual processing. It was not uncommon for anthropologists to reduce a body bag recovered from Ground Zero into as many as 100 new cases."[26]

Many fragments were so small that they could not be immediately identified as human. In these cases, the remains were considered human until further testing could either confirm or deny their origin. After triage, the remains that were conclusively human were sent on to the next stage of the process: identification.

Analyzing DNA

One of the most important advances forensic science has made in recent years is the ability to extract and analyze DNA. While such traditional methods as fingerprinting have been used for years by law enforcement agencies, authorities cannot always retrieve usable prints. For the forensic scientists trying to identify the victims of the 9/11 attacks, this was one of those times.

DNA, or deoxyribonucleic acid, is a molecule inside the nucleus of most cells in living organisms. DNA carries the genetic information that defines each individual organism; it is essentially a genetic blueprint. No two people (not even twins) have exactly the same DNA, which makes it an ideal substance for use in forensic identification. In addition, investigators need only a tiny portion of a person, such as a strand

By the Numbers

1.4 MILLION

Tons of rubble removed from Ground Zero.

of hair, a small sample of body fluid, or a minute piece of skin or bone, to collect enough DNA for identification purposes. This is a key advantage in disasters such as 9/11, where massive destruction makes whole bodies difficult to find.

Robert Shaler, director of the forensic biology department at the OCME, was in charge of the DNA identification program for the World Trade Center victims. His team began processing DNA samples the day after the attacks. He recalls:

Forensic specialists analyzed material found in the debris of the towers, such as these watches, for DNA to help identify victims.

> In those chaotic, early days when I was feeling the pressure to begin testing, I came to realize how important DNA would be for identifying most of those who died. . . . By Wednesday the disaster teams were in full swing, working two twelve-hour shifts accessioning [cataloging new samples], processing, and extracting DNA from specimens almost as quickly as they arrived.[27]

Even with twenty-four-hour workdays, the amount of material to be analyzed was overwhelming. But help soon arrived in the form of disaster mortuary operational response teams (DMORTs). Coordinated by the federal government, DMORTs respond to disasters when requested by the local community. The teams are made up of funeral directors, medicolegal investigators, pathologists, and other skilled civilian volunteers. Within days after the 9/11 attacks, DMORT personnel began arriving to help with the processing of DNA at both the OCME and the Pennsylvania crash site of Flight 93.

Two Kinds of DNA

DNA is found in almost all human cells. The vast majority of the DNA is found in the nucleus of the cell and is therefore called nuclear DNA. But there is another form of DNA, called mitochondrial DNA, which resides outside of the nucleus. This type of DNA is found in cellular mitochondria, tiny rodlike structures within the cell that help create enzymes that power the cell. Nuclear DNA contains more genetic information than mitochondrial DNA does. But mitochondrial DNA contains hundreds of copies of this information (nuclear DNA contains only two). Each type has its own particular advantages in forensic investigation.

A person inherits nuclear DNA from both of his or her parents. Mitochondrial DNA comes from the mother only. That makes this kind of DNA ideal for identifying a person through the mother's lineage. Mitochondrial DNA is also useful for identification of decomposed remains or those nearly destroyed in disasters, because the numerous copies of the genetic material it contains are more likely to provide a useable sample. Nuclear DNA is used in most forensic investigations because it is extremely accurate and results in very few false identifications.

It had been estimated that the recovery of remains from Ground Zero might take as long as a year to complete. This presented a potentially serious problem for the scientists working on DNA identification. Over time DNA can deteriorate, eventually making it impossible to extract usable samples for analysis. In addition, environmental conditions and the heat from the fires still burning at Ground Zero were already working to damage some of the DNA yet to be recovered. "If the thousands of tissues we would receive were badly decomposed," commented Shaler, "I wondered how effective DNA testing would be in identifying people. These fears became reality too quickly. Within a couple of weeks, the tissues were showing signs of extensive decomposition."[28] To speed up the process, investigators began using a robotic system to extract DNA samples. The robotic system could extract forty-four DNA samples at once, faster than technicians could do the work, and without the human involvement that might lead to contamination or mix-ups.

Information: Before and After Death

By itself, DNA extracted from recovered remains was not enough to identify a victim; it provided only half of the puzzle. To complete the identification process, the recovered DNA needed to be matched with another sample known to be from a particular person. The two halves of this DNA puzzle are called postmortem and antemortem information. Shiya Ribowsky, who had investigated numerous criminal cases for the OCME, knew that the scope of this situation was unprecedented:

> I realized, almost at once, that we were about to be flooded with what amounted to information from two different sources: the postmortem (data from the remains themselves), and the antemortem (descriptions and details about the victims provided by their family members). As in a death investigation, it would be

our job to combine everything we learned from both those sources to enable us to identify each victim. Only now we would be doing so with thousands of victims at once.[29]

By Wednesday, antemortem samples began arriving, brought to the OCME by relatives and friends. These included toothbrushes, hairbrushes, razors, articles of clothing, and even envelopes that a person may have licked to seal. These reference samples, called exemplars, were likely to contain DNA of a person listed as missing. People also brought in photos, dental records, descriptions of jewelry or tattoos, and anything else that might help in identifying physical remains. In many cases samples of DNA were taken from blood relatives of the missing persons. These samples were usually obtained by an oral swab, in which a cotton swab is rubbed across the inside of a person's cheek to remove cells that can be examined for their DNA. Such "kinship samples," while not exact matches to a relative's DNA, will nevertheless have enough markers in common with the missing person's DNA that an identification can be made.

Pentagon Casualties

When American Airlines Flight 77 struck the Pentagon, it smashed a hole nearly 100 feet (30.5m) wide in the west side of the building at approximately the first-floor level. As with the Twin Towers, burning jet fuel created a raging inferno that sent a huge fireball and oily black smoke hundreds of feet into the sky. Destruction of support columns inside the Pentagon caused the area above the point of impact to collapse about forty minutes after the crash. This delay allowed hundreds of workers on the upper floors of the five-story building to escape.

The crash killed 125 Pentagon workers (both military and civilian), as well as the 59 passengers and crew aboard Flight 77. The loss of life would have been greater had the Pentagon not been so sturdily built; its brick and concrete construction limited the damage made by the plane. In addition, the

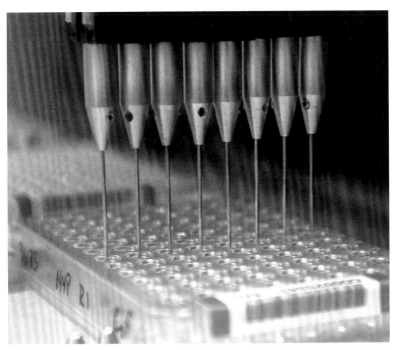

DNA samples found at Ground Zero were compared to samples such as toothbrushes and hairbrushes that were brought to the OCME by family members and friends.

area where the plane hit had been recently renovated and was not fully staffed on September 11. Of the 20,000 people in the building on that day, almost all were safely evacuated through the numerous exits located throughout the building. However, a total of 184 lives were lost in the 9/11 attack on the Pentagon.

Recovery and Identification

Recovery teams consisting of FBI agents, representatives of the Federal Emergency Management Agency, and military personnel searched the wreckage for bodies and body parts. When remains were found they were placed in body bags, removed from the wreckage, and carried to a temporary morgue that the FBI had set up in the Pentagon's north parking lot. Recovery soon became an around-the-clock operation, with soldiers and FBI agents working twelve-hour shifts. In addition to bodies, tons of rubble were deposited in the parking lot to be sifted for remains and personal effects.

Forensic odontologists (like the expert pictured here) studied the teeth of victims and compared them with dental records.

At the temporary morgue, remains were photographed and tagged with an identifying number. Then they were prepared to be flown to the Dover Port Mortuary at Dover Air Force Base in Delaware. Dover is the largest military mortuary in the United States and the main facility for receiving deceased military personnel and civilian defense workers. It would now be the primary facility for identifying the Pentagon victims from the 9/11 attacks. According to Armed Forces Institute of Pathology director Glenn Wagner, the task was "one of the most comprehensive forensic investigations in U.S. history."[30] Among the hundreds of people assembled at Dover were fifty military medical examiners and fifty FBI investigators.

When remains were brought to Dover, the initial stage of processing was to see if the hands were intact enough to obtain clear fingerprints, the easiest way to identify a body. Photographs were taken and compared to existing records of military and civilian employees. Forensic odontologists (dentists specializing in the examination of dental evidence for legal cases) studied the teeth of victims in order to make a comparison with dental records. Since teeth are the hardest parts of the human body, they hold up well in catastrophic accidents where other tissues and even bones are destroyed. The odontologists employed a computer program called WinID, which aids in dental identification and matching. Forensic odontology was the sole method of identification of sixty-five of the Pentagon victims.

Forensic radiology was also employed in the Pentagon identification process. X-rays were taken of intact bodies and body parts and compared with antemortem X-ray records. X-rays can reveal such evidence as broken bones that have healed, which can be valuable in the identification process. This was especially helpful in cases where dental records or DNA samples could not be obtained. Radiologists also were able to X-ray pieces of rubble to determine if any body parts or personal effects were present.

After two months of around-the-clock effort, the identification of the Pentagon victims of the 9/11 attacks came to an end. Only five of the victims could not be identified. The task now became the preparation of remains for return to their families for burial. Military deceased were dressed in the proper uniforms, with Purple Heart medals attached, and placed in caskets. Civilian remains were prepared with similar respect and dignity.

Pennsylvania

It did not look like the scene of an airplane crash. Wallace Miller, the coroner of Somerset County, Pennsylvania, arrived on the scene about forty minutes after United Flight 93 crashed into a field in Shanksville. The crater was still smoking and looked, according to Miller, "like someone took a scrap truck, dug a 10-foot ditch and dumped all this trash into it. . . . I stopped being coroner after about 20 minutes, because there were no bodies there."[31] It took about an hour of searching before Miller found a piece of human remains—the first of only fifteen hundred pieces recovered. Soon the area, designated a crime scene like the World Trade Center and the Pentagon, was teeming with FBI, fire department, police, and DMORT personnel. Over the next two weeks, some 600 pounds (272kg) of remains were retrieved and sent to a temporary morgue in

The crash site of Flight 93 was not much more than a smoldering crater in a field.

a National Guard armory about 10 miles (16km) from the crash site. Teams of forensic anthropologists, pathologists, and DNA experts worked to identify the remains of Flight 93's passengers and crew. Due to the extreme destruction of the crash, most identifications were made by DNA analysis. Remains that could not be identified at the temporary morgue were sent to the Dover Port Mortuary for further examination. By December 19, 2001, all forty of the passengers and crew of Flight 93 (with the exception of the hijackers) had been identified, thanks to the work of forensic scientists.

Somber Statistics

On September 11, 2001, 2,974 innocent lives were destroyed by the worst act of terrorism ever perpetrated on U.S. soil. The fatalities (not including the hijackers) included 2,750 killed in the World Trade Center (including all those aboard Flights 11 and 175), 184 in the Pentagon (including passengers and crew of Flight 77), and 40 in the crash of Flight 93 in Shanksville, Pennsylvania. Although 293 whole bodies were recovered, most remains found were small fragments of tissue and bone.

The identification process of the 9/11 victims ended in February 2005. Using the most modern forensic investigation techniques, scientists were able to identify 1,591 of the 9/11 victims. Of that total, 86 percent were identified by DNA analysis alone. Charles Hirsch, New York's chief medical examiner, wrote, "Without modern DNA technology we would have identified only 741 [World Trade Center] victims; 844 families that now have identification would have none, and we would have no hope of making additional identifications."[32] But there are limits on what technology can do. Some ten thousand bone fragments from the Twin Towers remained unidentified at New York's OCME.

Not listed in these statistics are nineteen other people: the hijackers. Who were they, and how could they have committed such a horrific act?

CHAPTER THREE

Identifying the Terrorists

Special Agent Kenneth Williams of the FBI office in Phoenix was concerned. He knew that several Middle Eastern men were taking flying lessons at flight schools in Arizona. He also knew that at least one of the men had connections with a terrorist group known as al Qaeda. Williams wrote a memo to FBI headquarters, reporting "an inordinate number of individuals of investigative interest who are attending or who have attended civil aviation universities and colleges in the State of Arizona." He believed "that a coordinated effort is underway to establish a cadre of individuals who will one day be working in the civil aviation community around the world. These individuals will be in a position in the future to conduct terror activity against civil aviation targets."[33]

Williams sent the memo on July 10, 2001. No one in the FBI did anything about it.

Death to America

In the Arabic language, *al Qaeda* means "the foundation" or "the base." It is the name given to a group of extreme Muslim radicals devoted to the expansion of the Muslim faith by any means necessary, including violence. Since its beginning in Afghanistan in 1988, al Qaeda has grown into a worldwide terrorist organization. In 1998 the organization issued a statement saying that all Muslims were duty bound to kill all Americans and their allies anywhere in the world. A network of terrorist "cells" operates around the world to carry out al Qaeda's mandate. Training camps established in Afghanistan are used to train al Qaeda operatives, and the organization supplies funds and weapons to support its terror operations.

The driving force behind al Qaeda was its founder, Osama bin Laden, a member of a wealthy Saudi Arabian family. In 1979 Bin Laden went to Afghanistan to raise money to fight against the Soviet Union, which had invaded that country earlier in the year. In 1988, as defeated Soviet troops were withdrawing from Afghanistan, Bin Laden left the country and founded al Qaeda. Soon al Qaeda began carrying out terror attacks on American interests, including the 1996 bombing of a Saudi apartment complex in which nineteen Americans died and an attack on the guided missile destroyer USS *Cole* in 2000 that killed seventeen American sailors.

In 1998 Bin Laden agreed to fund a mission proposed by one of his colleagues, Khalid Sheikh Muhammad. The plan was to hijack several commercial airliners and crash them into American buildings. As the plan unfolded, targets were determined: the World Trade Center, the Pentagon, the White House, and the U.S. Capitol. The plot, known as the "planes operation" within al Qaeda, originally envisioned ten aircraft striking targets in various U.S. cities. Eventually, the planners reduced the number of suicide planes to four. A group of Muslim radicals from a cell in Hamburg, Germany, became the core members of the 9/11 plot. Among them was a thirty-three-year-old Egyptian named Muhammad Atta.

Al Qaeda leader Osama bin Laden funded the terrorist plot to crash planes into American buildings.

Learning to Fly

Atta had not always been a radical Muslim. That began to change in 1992 when he moved to Hamburg to study engineering. There he became more religious and more extremist in his religious views. Atta attended the al Quds mosque in Hamburg, and after listening to much inflammatory preaching, his hatred

The Huffman Aviation Company did not realize it was training two of the terrorists who would later crash into the World Trade Center.

for America grew. He and several young men he met there eventually formed the core group of 9/11 terrorists: Atta, Ramzi Binalshibh, Marwan al-Shehhi, and Ziad Jarrah. Atta was a few years older than the others and soon became the leader. Kay Nehm, a German federal prosecutor, recalls, "He was considered the boss of the group on grounds of his age, his longer stay in Germany and the resulting good language skills, but also on grounds of his organizing talents and his persuasiveness."[34]

The exact steps in the planning of the attacks will never be fully known, but in early 2000, Atta sent an e-mail to between fifty and sixty flight schools in the United States. The e-mail read: "Dear sir, we are a small group of young men from different Arab countries. Now we are living in Germany since a while for study purposes. We would like to start training for the career of airline professional pilots. In this field we haven't yet any knowledge but we are ready to undergo an intensive training program."[35]

By June 2000 Atta, al-Shehhi, and Jarrah had entered the United States. Binalshibh made several attempts to join them but was denied an entry visa. He would, however, support the 9/11 plot by sending money to the hijackers. Atta and al-Shehhi enrolled at Huffman Aviation in Venice, Florida, for flight training. Jarrah also went to Venice, enrolling in a similar course at Florida Flight Training Center. At the end of 2000, they had received their commercial pilot licenses. The three "pilot hijackers" also trained on Boeing flight simulators, which gave them practice flying commercial airliners. During their training Atta and al-Shehhi expressed an interest in learning how to make turns and approaches with an aircraft, but not in other essential aspects of flying, such as takeoffs and landings. While this did not seem to alarm anyone at the fight schools, it fit into the terrorists' plans. The skills of taking off and landing were not necessary for the terrorists to hijack an aircraft in midflight and crash it into a building.

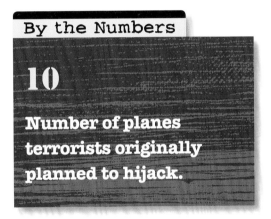

By the Numbers

10

Number of planes terrorists originally planned to hijack.

Completing the Teams

The fourth pilot was a twenty-nine-year-old named Hani Hanjour. Born in Saudi Arabia, Hanjour had lived on and off in the United States for ten years. After his first visit to the United States in October 1989, Hanjour became a changed man. According to one of his brothers, he "wore a full beard, cut his past social ties, and spent most of his time reading books on religion and airplanes."[36] Hanjour took flying lessons in Arizona and received his commercial pilot's license in 1999. Although he was not a very good pilot and had difficulty with the English language, Hanjour would pilot the fourth hijacked aircraft.

The terrorists knew that it would take more than pilots to commandeer a commercial aircraft. They needed accomplices who would be able to assault the cockpits, overpower the pilots, and make sure the passengers would not interfere

These nineteen hijackers carried out the 9/11 attacks: four were pilots and fifteen were muscle hijackers meant to overpower the crew and passengers.

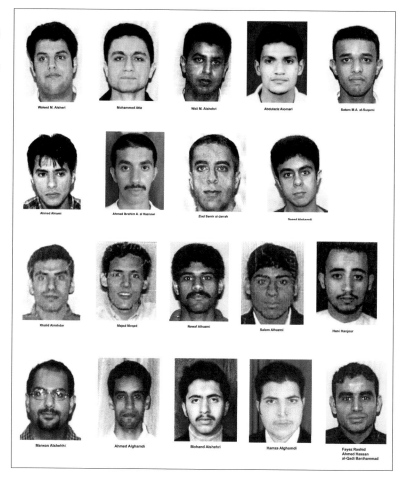

with the hijackings. These so-called muscle hijackers arrived in the United States between April and June 2001. They came from Saudi Arabia and the United Arab Emirates, and all were Islamic militants who had been trained in terrorist tactics at al Qaeda camps in Afghanistan. While they were eager to participate in a jihad, or holy war, against the West, they most likely did not know the details of the 9/11 plot. According to George Tenet, director of the Central Intelligence Agency (CIA), "they probably were told little more than that they were headed for a suicide mission inside the United States."[37]

The total number of terrorists actually to carry out the 9/11 attacks came to nineteen: four pilot hijackers and fifteen muscle hijackers. It was speculated that Ramzi Binalshibh was to be a twentieth hijacker. When he was denied entry into the United States, several others may have been considered, but the role of the twentieth hijacker (if it even existed) was never filled.

During the summer of 2001 the hijackers kept busy. "With their training complete," said FBI director Robert Mueller, "it appears that the pilots began conducting possible surveillance flights as passengers aboard cross-country flights transiting between the Northeast United States and California."[38] This allowed them to observe important details about the flights: where the flight attendants sat and how they performed their duties, how difficult it would be to break into the cockpit, and what the best time would be to begin the hijackings.

In the late summer of 2001, these nineteen young men were in the United States, living quietly in Florida and New Jersey. On the surface they appeared to be ordinary American citizens. "They dressed and acted like Americans," said Mueller, "shopping and eating at places like Wal-Mart and Pizza Hut."[39] But beneath that all-American facade hid the souls of nineteen Islamic radicals ready to kill, and die, for their beliefs. After the 9/11 attacks, questions swirled around Washington and the nation. Why were the attacks not prevented? Where was the U.S. intelligence community when Middle Eastern immigrants were learning to fly, but not land, commercial aircraft? The answers, not always satisfying ones, would eventually come.

Able Danger

On June 27, 2005, U.S. representative Curt Weldon stepped onto the floor of the House of Representatives and made a startling revelation to the members. "Mr. Speaker," Weldon began, "I rise because information has come to my attention over the past several months that is very disturbing. I have learned that, in fact, one of our Federal agencies had, in fact, identified the major New York cell of Mohamed Atta prior to

9/11."[40] Weldon stated further that the agency was prevented from sharing that information with the FBI, thus losing an opportunity to arrest Atta and perhaps prevent the 9/11 attacks. Could the U.S. government have known the identities of some of the hijackers before 9/11?

The agency Weldon referred to was called Able Danger, a secret military operation designed to collect information on suspected terrorist cells in the United States, including those with connections to al Qaeda. Begun in October 1999, Able Danger gathered its information using an investigative technique called data mining. In data mining, powerful computers are used to sift through the vast amount of data that exist in our modern world and then turn that data into useful information. For example, a store can look at a customer's purchasing history and suggest various products that the customer might be interested in. Law enforcement agencies can use data mining to uncover patterns or trends in crimes that could better prepare them for future criminal investigations. In terrorism investigations, looking at such data as telephone and real estate rental records could link suspected terrorists to others or to international terrorist organizations such as al Qaeda.

Weldon's information had come from several officers who had been in Able Danger before it was disbanded in January 2001. Several officers in the program stated that they had seen a chart that included the names of several 9/11 hijackers and a photo of Muhammad Atta almost two years before the attacks. The news media had a field day with such a sensational story, claiming that the government could have used the Able Danger information to prevent 9/11.

In 2006 the Pentagon released a report of its investigation of the Able Danger claims. It determined that the officers who had said they remembered seeing the chart were not accurate

By the Numbers

$450,000

Approximate cost to al Qaeda of the 9/11 plot.

in their recollections. In addition, no corroborating information had ever come to light. The report stated, "We found no charts or other documentation created before 9/11 that contained a photograph or name of Mohamed Atta and was produced or possessed by the Able Danger team."[41]

It now seems clear that the U.S. government did not know the identity of the hijackers before 9/11. On September 12, 2001, such information would have been a valuable identification tool for law enforcement authorities. Lacking these facts, the job of identifying the terrorists fell to the forensic scientists.

United States representative Curt Weldon testifies before the Senate Judiciary Committee about the Pentagon's previous knowledge of 9/11 terrorist Muhammad Atta.

From the Rubble

Everyone knew it, but no one mentioned it. As recovery crews searched through the devastated remains of the World Trade Center, some of the human remains they found might belong, not to the innocent victims of the attacks, but to the terrorists themselves.

"Follow the Money"

Along with the forensic investigation of the 9/11 attacks, the FBI pursued another avenue in its effort to identify the terrorists: It began tracing the money used to fund the attacks. FBI deputy assistant director J.T. Caruso outlined these activities for the House of Representatives on October 3, 2001:

> In addition to potential evidence collected at the scenes of these attacks, the FBI is working tirelessly to "follow the money" associated with the 19 hijackers. In the investigation of any terrorist organization, identifying and tracing funds used to finance and fund the organizations is a critical step. "Following the money" plays a key role in identifying those involved in criminal activity, establishing links among them, and developing evidence of their involvement in the activity. Locating, seizing, and/or freezing assets tied to terrorist organizations plays a key role in cutting off the financial lifeblood of these organizations and in not only dismantling the organization, but in preventing future terrorist acts. Due to the international nature of terrorist organizations, these investigations require considerable coordination with foreign authorities as well as the CIA and the Intelligence Community to ensure that the criminal investigation does not jeopardize or adversely impact sensitive national security matters. This requires careful adherence to restrictions separating criminal investigations from those involving national security and classified intelligence matters.

Quoted in Congressional Testimony of J.T. Caruso, Deputy Assistant Director, Counterterrorism Division, FBI, Before the House Intelligence Subcommittee on Terrorism and Homeland Defense, October 3, 2001. Federal Bureau of Investigation Web Site. www.fbi.gov/congress/congress01/caruso100301.htm.

Of course, there was no way for the recovery workers at Ground Zero to know the identity of the fragments they recovered. That would be up to the forensic investigators. At first, Robert Shaler of the OCME despaired of ever separating the hijackers' remains from those of the victims. In fact, he felt that there might not be any DNA from the hijackers at all. "I believed the crash and subsequent explosion had blasted them into tiny bits and pieces, most of which had probably vaporized in the ensuing fireball."[42] As the amount of human remains coming into the OCME increased, Shaler began thinking that perhaps finding fragments of the hijackers was possible. But recovering the fragments was one thing; being able to identify them was something else.

The difficulty was in how to make a positive identification without exemplars from the terrorists' relatives to match with the recovered fragments. It was not likely that anyone having a connection with the hijackers would come forward and reveal such an association. Khaled Abou El Fadl, a professor at the University of California at Los Angeles and an expert on Islamic law, said, "I've heard many times in the Muslim community that to claim and bury a body of one of the hijackers is to admit or accept that it was indeed those hijackers who committed 9/11."[43] This attitude reflected the belief of many Muslims that America itself had masterminded the 9/11 attacks to provide a justification for eventually invading Iraq. Without cooperation from the relatives of the hijackers, it seemed that the identification of their remains would be impossible. Then it occurred to Shaler that the FBI might have collected items belonging to suspected terrorists during their investigation. Early in 2002 Shaler contacted the FBI with his request and then waited for a reply.

PENTTBOM

Alan Giusti was in charge of the FBI's forensic investigation of the 9/11 attacks. When he received Shaler's request, his office was already processing physical evidence tentatively linked

The FBI looked for physical evidence of the hijackers at Ground Zero and the Fresh Kills landfill.

to men suspected of being the hijackers. The FBI's effort to identify the terrorists began within hours of the World Trade Center collapse. More than 7,000 FBI employees, including some 250 crime lab personnel, worked on the investigation, which was code-named PENTTBOM (Pentagon/Twin Towers Bombing Investigation). They conducted hundreds of interviews and tracked thousands of leads, coordinating their search with their counterparts in foreign countries. They collected physical evidence from Ground Zero and the Fresh Kills landfill, as well as from other locations where the terrorists had been.

Making the FBI's job somewhat easier was the fact that the hijackers did not use aliases: They used their real names on passports, credit card applications, and airline tickets purchased for the September 11 flights. They also were among the few passengers on the flights with Arabic names. In addition to this evidence, investigators discovered three identical copies of a letter written in Arabic. These were found in Muhammad Atta's suitcase (which did not make it onto Flight 11), in a vehicle that another hijacker had parked at Washington's Dulles Airport, and in the debris of Flight 93 in Shanksville, Pennsylvania. Translation of the letter revealed that it gave final instructions and offered prayers and encouragement to the hijackers. It read, in part:

> Make an oath to die and renew your intentions. . . . Pray for yourself and all your brothers that they may be victorious and hit their targets and ask God to grant you martyrdom facing the enemy, not running away from it. . . . When the confrontation begins, strike like champions who do not want to go back to this world. . . . Either end your life while praying, seconds before the target, or make your last words: "There is no God but God, Muhammad is His messenger". Afterwards, we will all meet in the highest heaven, God willing.[44]

Within three days of the attacks, the FBI had the names of the nineteen suspected hijackers. Investigators also determined that the terrorists came from four Middle Eastern countries: Saudi Arabia, the United Arab Emirates, Lebanon, and Egypt. At this point, the hijackers were classified as suspected terrorists. Their identities still had to be confirmed.

Evidence from the Terrorists

Ground Zero and Fresh Kills were not the only locations where evidence of the hijackers could be found. At FBI headquarters Giusti and his staff were looking for minute traces of DNA on items that the hijackers had left behind before they carried out the 9/11 plot. Agents searched hotel rooms, rental

The Twentieth Hijacker?

Nineteen terrorists took part in the 9/11 attacks. But were there supposed to be an even twenty hijackers? Speculation has run rampant on that topic and has centered on one man: Zacarias Moussaoui.

Zacarias Moussaoui was born in France in 1968 and, along with three siblings, raised by his mother. After receiving a master's degree, Moussaoui began associating with Islamic radicals, eventually receiving training at al Qaeda camps in Afghanistan. In February 2001 he entered the United States and began taking flying lessons in Oklahoma. He flunked out of that flight school but later took lessons on a commercial airliner simulator in Minnesota. His instructor there became suspicious of his lack of piloting skills and called the FBI. Moussaoui was arrested in August 2001 for an immigration violation.

After 9/11 it was believed that Moussaoui was a part of the plot, so he was tried in federal court. He was convicted of conspiracy to commit terrorism and sentenced to life in prison. He resides at a maximum security facility in Colorado.

Was Zacarias Moussaoui the twentieth hijacker? In court he stated that he was not involved with 9/11, explaining that he had been planning another attack on the United States. While we may never know the truth, we can take comfort in the fact that he will never be free to turn his plan into a terrible reality.

cars, and anywhere else the hijackers had been shortly before boarding the flights on 9/11. According to Giusti, they collected "fingernail clippings, chewing gum, hairbrushes, anything we could get dead skin off of."[45] Once the items from the hijackers were brought into the lab, the DNA was chemically extracted and analyzed. Then a "genetic map" for each sample was created, strings of numbers that were unique to a single person. In time Giusti's team isolated the DNA profiles of ten people suspected of being part of the 9/11 attacks.

More than a year after Shaler sent his request to the FBI, he finally received a written reply. The letter contained Giusti's DNA profiles on the ten suspected hijackers; no names, just a string of coded genetic information for each person. The information was entered into the OCME's DNA database, and immediately two matches were made. Here was the first positive identification of 9/11 terrorists. It was a breakthrough, but it also created a problem.

During the recovery operation at Ground Zero, Shaler met periodically with the families of the victims to provide progress reports. The relatives often asked if any of the hijackers had been identified. "They did not want terrorists mixed in with their loved ones," remarked Shaler. The hijackers "were criminals and did not deserve to be with them."[46] Shaler shared the families' sympathies and ordered the hijackers' fragments separated from the rest of the remains.

Shanksville and the Pentagon

Unlike the World Trade Center, where thousands of civilians were in the towers when the planes struck, the area where Flight 93 crashed in Shanksville, Pennsylvania, was an empty field. Discounting the unlikely possibility that someone had been in the field at the time of the crash, the remains at the site could only be from the passengers or the hijackers. It was a classic closed population disaster; the names of all those aboard Flight 93 could be learned from the passenger list.

The families of the Flight 93 passengers provided personal items to be used in matching DNA samples. In addition, a surprising number of undamaged personal effects were found among the wreckage. Seven boxes worth of items ranging from wedding rings to shoes, wallets, and photos were recovered, helping officials in the identification process. Within two weeks after the crash, sixteen of the victims had been identified through the use of dental records and fingerprints. The rest of the remains were so small and so decomposed that they had to be identified using DNA analysis.

For that task coroner Wallace Miller turned to the Armed Forces DNA Identification Laboratory (AFDIL) in Rockville, Maryland. A unit of the Armed Forces Institute of Pathology, AFDIL provides forensic DNA analysis services for the Department of Defense and other government agencies. "Our priority was not the hijackers," said Brion Smith, head of the lab, "it was getting the victims back to their families."[47] By December 11 all forty of the passengers and crew of Flight 93 had been identified. During the analysis, four DNA profiles were found that did not match any of the exemplars submitted by the families. By process of elimination, these

Personnel records helped investigators separate the victims' remains from the hijackers' remains.

Extracting DNA from Bones

1 Remove surface contaminants by washing and scraping the bone.

2 Using a bone saw, obtain a sample of the bone's core (marrow).

3 Pulverize the bone into powder. A nitrogen-filled mill is usually employed to reduce heat, which can destroy DNA.

4 Extract the DNA from the bone powder by mixing with an extraction buffer solution and placing in a centrifuge for several minutes.

5 Create numerous copies of the DNA by a process known as amplification.

6 Compare DNA to a known sample for identification.

were presumed to be the remains of the four hijackers who tried unsuccessfully to carry out their mission.

The military keeps thorough records on its personnel, including blood samples. This helped investigators at the Pentagon site positively to identify the military victims of the terrorist attack. As with Flight 93, no exemplars were provided for the remains of the hijackers, so identification of the five terrorists aboard Flight 77 was made by process of elimination. Matching the DNA from the presumed hijackers' remains with a Near Eastern genetic database confirmed that the five were from that area of the world. In addition, the investigators concluded that two of the hijackers were brothers.

In all, the remains of thirteen of the nineteen hijackers have been identified. According to an FBI spokesman, the terrorists' remains are "stored as evidence in a refrigerated locker in sealed containers and test tubes."[48] There they will remain as long as the 9/11 investigation remains open.

CHAPTER FOUR

Why the Towers Fell

On the morning of July 28, 1945, a U.S. Army Air Force B-25 twin engine bomber flew low through a dense fog that blanketed New York. The pilot was lost. At 9:40 A.M. the B-25 crashed into the seventy-ninth floor of New York's famous Empire State Building. The plane ripped an 18 by 20 foot (5.5 by 6 m) hole in the building's side, and its fuel tanks exploded, creating a massive fireball. Fourteen people died in the crash, including the plane's crew. Survivors had to walk down seventy flights of stairs to reach safety on the ground. Fortunately, the crash occurred on a Saturday when only fifteen hundred workers were there—about 10 percent of the building's weekday occupancy.

This 1945 air disaster at the Empire State Building held many similarities to the World Trade Center crashes fifty-six years later: the fiery collision, the smoke and flames, and the survivors walking down darkened stairways to safety. But one important difference stands out: the Empire State Building did not collapse. This fact raised a question that haunted engineers and architects: If a building constructed in the 1930s could withstand an airplane slamming into it, why did the ultramodern World Trade Center not survive?

A Design for Commerce

In September 1962 Minoru Yamasaki, a Japanese American architect, was hired to design a group of buildings in New York called the World Trade Center. It was a huge project estimated to cost $280 million, a staggering figure in the early 1960s. Undaunted, Yamasaki and his staff immediately went to work. "We're going to do this building," Yamasaki said. "It's

Architect Minoru Yamasaki was hired in 1962 to design the World Trade Center.

going to be the tallest in the world. It's going to be the grandest project ever."[49] Over the next fifteen months and more than one hundred design ideas, the final plan of the World Trade Center slowly emerged. Two square towers would dominate a 16-acre (6.5ha) plaza in lower Manhattan, towering over four other buildings on the site. The towers would be 110 stories each, high enough to accommodate the Port Authority's requirement of 10 million square feet (929,000 sq. m) of rentable space. This made them the tallest buildings in the world at the time. The towers would be clad in aluminum, which reflected different shades of light at various times of the day.

The job of turning Yamasaki's design into reality was given to the firm of Worthington, Skilling, Helle, and Jackson in Seattle, Washington, whose engineer Leslie Robertson would become lead structural engineer on the project. Robertson created a structure that was innovative while allowing the maximum amount of rentable space in the towers. Traditional skyscrapers such as the Empire State Building had always been constructed with a grid of steel columns that provided support for the building. The exterior walls simply afforded protection from the outside environment and allowed light in through the windows. While this made for a sturdy building, the forest of interior columns limited the amount of space that could be rented.

Robertson's design, however, shifted most of the load-bearing job to a series of steel columns that formed the outer walls of the towers. The close spacing of the columns was key to the integrity of the design. At just 3 feet, 4 inches (1m) apart, the columns would adequately support the tremendous weight of the towers. In the center of the buildings was a central core of elevators and stairways surrounded by more columns. This radical design resulted in nearly 1 acre (0.4ha) of rentable space on each floor. This was Robertson's, and the Port Authority's, goal: to create enough floor space to make the World Trade Center economically viable.

By the Numbers

200,000

Tons of steel used in World Trade Center construction.

Testing the Design

With such a revolutionary design, a good deal of testing needed to be done to assure the structural stability of the Twin Towers. One of the factors that Robertson examined was the effect of wind on the towers. The World Trade Center site was known to be one of the windiest in New York. In an 80-mile-per-hour (129km/h) wind, the Empire State Building swayed some 3.6 inches (9.1cm). After running computer models and wind tunnel tests on scale models of the towers, engineers calculated that the World Trade Center would sway anywhere from 10 to 14 inches (25 to 36cm) in a wind of similar velocity.

Not only must the buildings be able to withstand the wind, the people inside must remain comfortable as well. Psychologists performed tests to determine the comfort level of people working in skyscrapers. In these tests unsuspecting people were led into a room that was rigged to create motions simulating a building swaying in the wind. As the swaying was slowly increased, test subjects reported sensations ranging from being sick, to being on a boat, to being drunk. One subject thought her gravity was being taken away; another wondered if she was being hypnotized. The experiments showed that many people were sensitive to the slightest motion of a swaying building. Could people work in an environment where the building rocked back and forth about a foot (30.5cm)? A psychologist put it succinctly: "People will get used to almost anything."[50]

The World Trade Center under construction in 1970. It took seven years to build the World Trade Center.

Wind was not the only threat to the towers that the engineers had to consider. Mindful, perhaps, of the B-25 crash into the Empire State Building, structural engineers began studies to determine the effect of an aircraft hitting the World Trade Center. Their calculations centered on the largest airliner of the day, the Boeing 707. The engineers tried to determine the amount of force a 707 would exert upon striking one of the towers and whether this force could tip over the building. Their answer was 17 million pounds (7.7 million kg)—more than the force of a windstorm, but not enough to topple the building. They also considered the hole an airplane strike would create in the towers. Would such damage weaken the building to the point of collapse? What they found was that the World Trade Center's unique use of narrowly spaced exterior columns would actually help keep the building upright. In theory, if numerous columns were severed, the pressure exerted by the floors above the impact area would be distributed to the remaining columns, thus keeping the tower standing. Calculations indicated that even if all the columns on one side of a tower were destroyed, the building could still withstand a 100-mile-per-hour (161km/h) wind.

In February 1964, more than two years before construction began, a report was issued on the engineering design of the World Trade Center. It included the following section:

> The buildings have been investigated and found to be safe in an assumed collision with a large jet airliner (Boeing 707—DC 8) traveling at 600 miles per hour. Analysis indicates such collision would result in only local damage which could not cause collapse or substantial damage to the building and would not endanger the lives and safety of occupants not in the immediate area of impact.[51]

Engineer Leslie Robertson also performed calculations for a Boeing 707 crashing into the World Trade Center. Based on assumptions of a plane weighing 263,000 pounds (119,295kg) and traveling at 180 miles per hour (290km/h), Robertson concluded that the Twin Towers would be safe from an accidental airplane strike.

However, both studies seemed to disregard the consequences of fire damage. Based on the experience of the B-25 hitting the Empire State Building, the engineers knew that a fire was inevitable in such a crash. But the New York landmark had survived the impact and remained standing. The engineers believed that a fire in the World Trade Center, as terrible as it surely would be, would remain localized to the area of the crash. "Our analysis," recalled John Skilling of the World Trade Center project's engineering firm, "indicated the biggest problem would be the fact that all the fuel (from the airplane) would dump into the building. There would be a horrendous fire. A lot of people would be killed." But in spite of that, Skilling continued, "the building structure would still be there."[52]

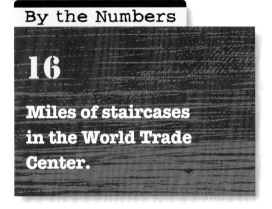

By the Numbers

16

Miles of staircases in the World Trade Center.

Despite their best calculations and intensive testing procedures, the 9/11 attacks tragically would prove the engineers wrong.

A Matter of Seconds

It took seven years to build the World Trade Center; it took just seconds for the towers to collapse into a pile of twisted rubble. Two World Trade Center, the south tower, was the second to be hit but the first to collapse. Struck by Flight 175 at 9:03 A.M., for nearly an hour that morning the upper floors of the tower were engulfed in thick black smoke. Then at 9:59 the building collapsed in a huge, descending cloud of smoke and debris. According to the National Institute of Standards and Technology (NIST), the collapse of the south tower took

W. Gene Corley, left, presents his findings to the House Committee on Science after investigating the World Trade Center towers' collapse.

only nine seconds. The north tower, although struck first, stood for 102 minutes before collapsing at 10:28, the destruction taking about eleven seconds. Why did the buildings disintegrate so quickly and so completely? Was there more at work than just the impacts of the airliners? Or was there perhaps a "fatal flaw" in the design of the World Trade Center? The American Society of Civil Engineers (ASCE) began an investigation to find out.

On the afternoon of September 11, the ASCE began to explore how to conduct the investigation, with assistance and financing from the Federal Emergency Management Agency. Building Performance Assessment Teams were established to study both the World Trade Center and Pentagon sites. W. Gene Corley, a structural engineer and expert on building collapses, was the ASCE's lead investigator for the World Trade Center inquiry. Corley was no stranger to building disasters, having investigated the 1995 bombing of the Murrah Federal Building in Oklahoma City. One hundred sixty-eight people were killed in that bombing, and the building suffered such extensive damage that it had to be torn down.

Expert assistance was requested from other organizations involved in the construction industry, including the

American Concrete Institute, the American Institute of Steel Construction, the National Fire Protection Association, and the Structural Engineers Association of New York. As in all criminal investigations, the first priority of the Trade Center investigators was to examine the evidence. But here Corley and his teams ran into their first obstacle.

Searching for Evidence

The logical place to start an investigation into why the towers collapsed was to examine the structural steel that had supported

Buried Treasure

When one thinks of buried treasure, images of pirate ships and buccaneers probably come to mind. But the World Trade Center also had its very own buried treasure. Huge bombproof vaults located beneath the World Trade Center held a fortune in gold and silver, owned by the Bank of Nova Scotia. After the collapse of the towers, the treasure was buried under tons of rubble.

Within the vaults lay thousands of gold and silver bars with an estimated worth of $200 million, although some reports placed the value at as much as $650 million. Such a huge sum would be a tempting target for criminals, and it was reported that scorch marks were seen on a vault door—evidence, perhaps, of an attempt to steal the riches. So officials in control of Ground Zero took no chances. Under the watchful eyes and automatic weapons of armed guards, police officers and firefighters began removing the precious metals. In all, some 379,036 ounces (10,745kg) of gold and 29,942,619 ounces (848,859kg) of silver were recovered from the vaults beneath Ground Zero. Eventually the World Trade Center treasure was transferred to other storage facilities, safe from would-be robbers.

the World Trade Center. In all there were some 300,000 tons (272,155t) of steel, including 90,000 tons (81,647t) from each tower, lying twisted and rusting at Ground Zero. To the engineers, these huge pieces of metal contained evidence that, when properly measured and analyzed, could provide valuable clues to the structural failure of the towers. But New York City officials apparently chose to disregard, or did not realize the importance of, this aspect of the investigation. Michael Bloomberg, who became New York's mayor in 2002, said: "If you want to take a look at the construction methods and the design, that's in this day and age what computers do. Just looking at a piece of metal generally doesn't tell you anything."[53]

Computer simulations are important, of course, but as an engineer Corley knew the value of being able to examine firsthand the actual remains from a building collapse. Unknown to Corley and his team, however, the city of New York had already begun shipping the steel across the Hudson River to several scrap yards in New Jersey. While this was not known to the general public, one of Corley's team members personally discovered what was taking place. On his first night in New York, engineering professor Abolhassan Astaneh-Asl looked out of his hotel window. On the street below he saw a parked truck filled with large pieces of steel. Going downstairs, Astaneh-Asl discovered that the steel came from Ground Zero and was being taken to the docks for transport to a New Jersey scrap yard. For several nights Astaneh-Asl studied the steel on trucks that parked at that same spot. "I've found quite a number of interesting items,"[54] Astaneh-Asl said.

When the steel reached the scrap yards, it would be cut into smaller pieces and shipped overseas to China, India, and other countries to be melted down and reused. Once that happened, any clues to the disaster that the steel could give investigators would be lost. "We thought they were going to be held for at least a while until we could get to them," commented Corley. "If they're recycling all of it, that would make it more difficult."[55] In fact, the ASCE had previously faxed a request to the city asking to inspect the steel, but the fax somehow went astray. The ASCE quickly submitted another request and received permission to examine the steel, although the recycling process would continue.

Stories in Steel

In an intense six-day investigation, Corley and his team walked through Ground Zero and the scrap yards, studying, measuring, and photographing the steel remnants of the World Trade Center. They were now forensic engineers looking for clues, however tiny or obscure, that might be hidden in the tons of rubble. Along with the on-site investigation, samples of the steel were collected and preserved for laboratory analysis. To the trained eyes of the engineers, the steel had a story to tell. "What we're looking for," said Corley as he examined the

Investigators studied the steel remnants of the World Trade Center to look for clues on why the buildings collapsed.

twisted beams, "is pieces that were in the areas where fires occurred. You can get a better idea of what the strength was before the collapse occurred."[56] The investigators were aided by numbers that had been etched into the steel before construction. They identified which tower a particular piece was from, and where in the tower it had been located.

The investigation eventually centered on the steel trusses that supported the 110 concrete floors in each of the towers. Unlike any previous skyscraper, the World Trade Center was built using trusses to support the floors. These trusses were lightweight structures consisting of two major horizontal beams connected with diagonal reinforcing bars. The result was a floor support as strong as ordinary steel beams, but much lighter in weight and cheaper to construct. As Corley's team examined the floor trusses, they were especially interested in the ends of the trusses, where they had been connected by bolts and weld joints to the outer support columns of the towers. What they found provided vital clues to the cause of the collapse: bolts that were bent or broken. The intense heat of the fires on the floors where the planes hit had caused the floor trusses to soften and sag. Structural engineer Charles Thornton explained:

> They had two ⅝-inch bolts at one end of the truss and two ¾-inch bolts at the other end, which is perfectly fine to take vertical load and perfectly fine to take shear [horizontal] loads, but once the floor elements start to sag during a fire . . . they start exerting tension forces because it becomes . . . like a clothesline, and those two little bolts just couldn't handle it.[57]

Fireproofing proved to be another element in the collapse of the Twin Towers. During construction the interior structural elements, including the trusses, had been coated with a foamlike fire retardant. According to one study of photographic evidence, over the years this material had deteriorated in some places and had not been properly repaired. When the planes hit the towers, the impacts were so violent that the fireproofing material was literally blown off the beams it was designed to protect. Without this fireproofing, the steel was left to the mercy of the flames.

Becoming a Forensic Engineer

Job Description:
Forensic engineers apply their backgrounds in various engineering fields to matters related to our judicial system. They may investigate fires, building collapses, roadway and bridge failures, industrial accidents, and product liability claims. Forensic engineers often testify as expert witnesses in civil and criminal court cases.

Education:
A minimum of a bachelor's degree in an engineering discipline is required.

Qualifications:
Experience in any of the various areas of engineering (civil, mechanical, structural, etc.) is necessary. Also important is the ability to conduct objective investigations, to work in potentially dangerous locations, and to testify in court accurately and concisely.

Additional Information:
Engineers may receive certification in forensic engineering by the National Academy of Forensic Engineers. Licensure as a professional engineer (PE) also may be beneficial.

Salary:
Engineering salaries vary widely, and can range from about $50,000 to over $100,000 annually.

Laboratory analysis of pieces of the steel trusses confirmed that the fires had reached some 2,000°F (1,093°C), enough to cause the trusses to weaken. Once the floor trusses began to sag, they could no longer carry the weight of the floors they were designed to support. As Astaneh-Asl said, "So now we know . . . it was a failure of the floor in most cases."[58] A thorough evaluation of the World Trade Center's structural steel had given the investigators a good idea of the cause of the towers' collapse. Examination of other evidence confirmed their hypothesis.

Video Evidence

There were numerous videos of the attacks that could be viewed to reveal structural damage and show exactly how the buildings fell.

One aspect that set the 9/11 attacks apart from other disasters was the amount of photographic coverage of the event. By the time the towers collapsed, there were untold numbers of cameras, both still and video, trained on the scene. Many of those cameras were from local and national television outlets, bringing the drama unfolding in New York into the homes of millions of viewers around the world. Countless more were

used by ordinary citizens intent on capturing a moment in history; still others were surveillance cameras, set up to monitor a portion of the city but coincidentally aimed toward the towers. "There is an enormous volume of video and photographic documentation of the events of September 11th," Corley said. "This type of evidence can often yield significant insights into the failure mechanisms."[59]

One piece of video footage, recorded by an architectural firm near the Twin Towers, revealed that the south tower had fallen away from the side where Flight 175 hit and toward the area where the fires were most intense. This confirmed to Corley that the fires, not merely the impact, had weakened the floor trusses and the outer support columns. When the trusses sagged, the force bent the weakened outer columns until they, too, failed, causing the tower to collapse.

Studying the video footage of the World Trade Center revealed that the north tower collapsed in a different manner. Topping the north tower was a 360-foot (110m) broadcast antenna, and the way it fell provided a clue to the collapse. "Looking at the films of the North Tower," recalled Corley, "it appears that the antenna starts down just a little bit before the exterior of the building. That suggests the core went first."[60] Flight 11 had struck the building almost head-on, destroying many of the load-bearing columns of the central core. Weakened by this massive structural damage and the fire, the core could no longer support the weight above it, and the collapse inevitably followed.

Another Look

Corley's inquiry into the collapse of the Twin Towers, completed in May 2002, was as thorough as he could make it. But many people, including industry experts and the families of the victims, felt that further investigation was warranted. In August 2002 NIST, a part of the U.S. Department of Commerce, began its own three-year investigation, funded with $16 million of federal money.

Leslie Robertson's Nightmare

Leslie Robertson, lead structural engineer for the World Trade Center project, is haunted by the tragic end of the buildings he so carefully designed. In an ironic coincidence, one of Robertson's office windows overlooks the site where the Twin Towers once stood. Robertson says:

> In my mind, the loss of life and the loss of the buildings are somehow separated. Thoughts of the thousands who lost their lives as my structures crashed down upon them come to me at night, rousing me from sleep, and interrupting my thoughts at unexpected times throughout the day. Those who were trapped above the impact floors, those who endured the intense heat only to be crushed by falling structure, are merged with those who chose to take control of their own destinies by leaping from the towers.
>
> The loss of the buildings is more abstract. The buildings represented about 10 years of concerted effort both in design and in construction on the part of talented men and women from many disciplines. It just isn't possible for me to take the posture that the towers were only buildings . . . that these material things are not worthy of grieving.
>
> Leslie E. Robertson, "Reflections on the World Trade Center," Bridge, National Academy of Engineering Publications, Spring, 2002. www .nae.edu/ nae/ bridgecom.nsf/ weblinks/ CGOZ-58NLCB.

Leslie Robertson was the lead structural engineer for the World Trade Center project. He is haunted by what happened on 9/11.

More than a thousand people were interviewed for the NIST study. These included technical experts from various disciplines; people involved in the design, construction, and maintenance of the World Trade Center; and many people who were on the scene on September 11, 2001. More than 200 pieces of steel were examined, along with 150 hours of video footage and almost 7,000 still photographs. Computer animations were an important part of the investigators' toolkit. Created by an outside contractor, the animations recreated the aircraft crashing into the towers, showing the damage the impacts caused to the structural elements. The computers displayed the trajectories of the fragments of both the airplanes and the buildings so that investigators could determine how the airplanes came apart and the extent of the damage they caused. Fuel spilled from the airplanes' tanks was also analyzed to determine where and how quickly the fires had spread. So detailed were these simulations that it took a bank of computers two weeks to create each animation. Investigators also built replicas of work stations typically used in World Trade Center offices, and then set them on fire to observe how the fires created by the crashes may have spread through the stricken buildings.

The NIST study concluded that the narrow spacing of the perimeter columns created a strong structure that withstood the initial aircraft impacts. In its final report, NIST stated that the towers would have remained standing if the foam fire insulation had not been dislodged by the crashes. As it was, the buildings performed well under the extreme conditions placed upon them, standing long enough to allow most of the fifteen thousand occupants below the impact floors to evacuate safely.

NIST's conclusions are the result of a thorough scientific study of the evidence. But not everyone accepts the facts presented by NIST or the thousands of other investigators, scientists, and technicians who worked so diligently in the aftermath of the terrorist attacks. Many people believe that something more sinister occurred on September 11, 2001, and that the U.S. government was involved in the destruction of the Twin Towers.

CHAPTER FIVE

Conspiracy?

The idea that four commercial airliners could be hijacked by terrorists and used as deadly weapons against the United States is difficult for many people to comprehend. The fact that it actually happened on September 11, 2001, is perhaps even more unbelievable. In the years following 9/11, most Americans came to grips with the most deadly attack ever carried out on U.S. soil. Countless books, articles, television programs, and official reports have presented the conclusions of expert investigators regarding the events of that September morning. But not everyone is satisfied with those conclusions. Newspaper columnist Richard Roeper explains:

> Before sunset on 9/11, conspiracy theorists were already working themselves into frenzied speculation about what was *really* going on. By now the 9/11 conspiracy game is an industry unto itself, with dozens of Web sites, DVDs, and books dedicated to "exposing" the "real truth" about what happened on that terrible day and who was "really" behind it.[61]

The Internet has become the main outlet for people promoting alternate theories of how, and by whom, the World Trade Center attacks were carried out. In 2006 one conspiracy Web site was receiving twelve thousand hits a day. Who are these conspiracy theorists, and what is the real truth they say they know about the 9/11 attacks?

Conspiracy 101

According to numerous conspiracy theorists, the 9/11 attacks were not committed by a group of nineteen Middle Eastern

Conspiracy theorists believe the war in Iraq was planned by the U.S. government years before the 9/11 attacks.

terrorists. They were part of a complicated plot hatched by the U.S. government to create a pretext for launching a war against one or more Middle Eastern nations. The war in Iraq was the result of this plot, the conspiracy theorists claim. This war had been in the planning stages by the U.S. government for many years before 2001, so the theory goes. When the international situation failed to create a reason to implement the plan, Washington created its own reason by staging the 9/11 attacks.

Besides war, some of the other reasons advanced by the theorists are that the government wanted to restrict the freedoms of U.S. citizens or to create a justification for increasing military spending. Some conspiracy theorists believe that the 9/11 attacks were indeed committed by the terrorists, but that the U.S. government knew about the hijacking plan and allowed it to happen. Most, however, believe that the official story of the attacks, including the results of the forensic investigations that followed, are mere fabrications designed to cover up the true nature of the tragedy. The idea that the truth about 9/11 is being covered up is sometimes referred to as the "9/11 Truth Movement." Many individuals and organizations consider themselves members of this movement, searching for the truth that they say is hidden behind a wall of government deception and even criminal actions.

By the Numbers

36

The percentage of Americans who believe the U.S. government was involved in, or had advance knowledge of, the 9/11 attacks.

Numerous books, radio programs, and videos promote the 9/11 Truth Movement. One conspiracy video titled *Loose Change* has been viewed millions of times on the Internet site YouTube.

To impart authenticity to their ideas, the conspiracy theorists perform their own investigations of some of the 9/11 evidence. Their conclusions, however, are usually at odds with the results of the official inquiries.

Melting Steel

One of the most frequent claims made by the conspiracy theorists is that the fires caused by the airliners impacting the World Trade Center were not hot enough to melt the steel structural supports of the towers. Since the steel did not melt, then the plane crashes could not be the explanation for the towers' collapse. As evidence, the theorists begin by stating that until 9/11 no skyscraper has ever collapsed due to fire damage. "We have been lied to," states Jerry Russell on the Web site AttackOnAmerica.net. "We have been lied to about this, at multiple levels. The first lie was that the load of fuel from the aircraft was the cause of structural failure. No kerosene [a component of aviation fuel] fire can burn hot enough to melt steel."[62]

The melting point of steel is about 2,912°F (1,600°C), and it is true that ordinary fires only reach a temperature of about 2,012°F (1,100°C). But that is beside the point: The steel in the World Trade Center did not have to melt in order to cause the collapse of the towers. It only had to reach a temperature where it became so weak that it lost its ability to support the buildings. According to NIST: "At temperatures of about 300°C, steel loses about 20% of its yield strength.... At temperatures above 500°C, the steel further weakens, loss of strength and stiffness become significant, and the column's ability to carry its share of the building loads decreases."[63]

Some conspiracy theorists believe that the fires caused by the planes were not hot enough to melt the steel structural supports of the towers. As a result, they feel the plane crashes could not be the explanation for the towers' collapse.

Computer simulations performed by NIST calculated the heat inside the impact floors at between 932°F (500°C) and 1,832°F (1,000°C). In addition, the destruction of much of the sprayed-on fireproofing on these floors by the planes' impacts left the steel vulnerable to the heat of the fires. The temperatures were more than enough to heat the structural elements in the towers, especially the lightweight floor trusses, to the point of losing their structural strength.

Although scientific testing proved that the steel in the World Trade Center could weaken without melting, the conspiracy theorists had another idea as to why the towers fell. And it had nothing to do with airplanes.

Demolition

Most people are familiar with controlled demolition, in which old or condemned buildings are destroyed by explosives strategically placed by expert demolitionists. Television news broadcasts often show famous structures collapsing, seemingly in slow motion, brought down by charges ignited with split-second precision. As the numerous video clips of the Twin Towers collapsing seem to show, their destruction appeared eerily like a controlled demolition. And so the conspiracy theorists claim that the World Trade Center was destroyed, not by hijacked airliners, but by explosive charges placed in the towers prior to September 11, 2001.

Statements by eyewitnesses show that many people thought the buildings were being purposely destroyed. Beth Fertig, a news reporter for a New York radio station, recalled, "The tower went down perfectly straight, as if a demolition crew had imploded it."[64] ABC television reporter Don Daylor commented on the air as he watched the south tower collapse: "The second building that was hit by the plane has just completely collapsed. The entire building has just collapsed, as if a demolition team set off—when you see the old demolitions of these old buildings. It folded down on itself, and it's not there any more."[65] Even some experts acknowledged the similarity.

Architectural engineer Matthys Levy stated: "It was very much like a controlled demolition when you look at it, because the building essentially fell almost vertically down, as if someone had deliberately set a blast to take place to cause the building to fall vertically downward."[66]

If it looked like a controlled demolition, then it must be a controlled demolition—at least, that is what the conspiracy theorists argue. As evidence, they cite video footage of the towers collapsing, which shows puffs of smoke emanating from the sides of the buildings as they fall, an indication of explosives going off. And yet there is another explanation for those puffs of smoke. To professional investigators, they can be logically explained by the fact that the upper floors exerted an enormous force on the floors below as they collapsed. This created tremendous air pressure on the floors below that blew

Conspiracy theorists think the smoke coming from the sides of the south tower, shown here collapsing, is an indication of a controlled demolition.

out windows and sent pulverized debris shooting out of the sides of the towers, giving the appearance of explosions. Shyam Sunder, an NIST investigator, explains that "when you have a significant portion of the floor collapsing, it's going to shoot air and concrete dust out the window."[67] *Popular Mechanics* magazine, which began investigating 9/11 conspiracy theories in 2004, consulted with professional demolition experts. These experts also rejected the notion that controlled demolition could have brought down the World Trade Center. "There's just no way to do it," explained Mark Loizeau, head of a leading demolition company. He says that manufacturing processes to make explosive charges that could have destroyed the towers does not exist. "If someone were to attempt to make such charges, they would weigh thousands of pounds apiece. You would need forklifts to bring them into the building."[68]

The Mysterious Pod

The video evidence for two airliners striking the World Trade Center is plentiful. Yet even here the conspiracy theorists stand at odds with the official investigations. One problem the theorists see is that the hijackers were poor pilots, incapable of guiding a Boeing 767 into the Twin Towers with such pinpoint accuracy. The Web site *9-11 Review* states: "None of the alleged hijackers were good pilots, and none had flown jet airplanes, let alone large jetliners. Yet they are supposed to have piloted jetliners into small targets. The maneuvers of the jet that targeted the Pentagon required top-gun piloting, *if they were even humanly possible*."[69]

How then, do the conspiracy theorists explain the accuracy of the 9/11 flights? They contend that the planes were flown, not by the hijackers, but by remote control. Video footage of Flight 175 moments before it crashed into the south tower seems to show a bulge underneath the plane. This is usually referred to as a "pod" by conspiracy theorists and is said by some to contain remote control equipment. Their theory is that by using this equipment, U.S. government operatives were

Project Northwoods

In 1959 Fidel Castro became the dictator of Cuba, turning the island nation into a Communist stronghold just 90 miles (144.8km) from the Florida coast. It was the height of the Cold War, and Castro's regime presented a clear and present danger to the United States. In 1962 the Joint Chiefs of Staff, America's military leaders, drafted a plan called Operation Northwoods. Under this plan American intelligence operatives would stage acts of terrorism against the United States and blame them on Cuba. This would provide a pretext for military strikes against Cuba and the downfall of Castro. The terrorism envisioned included bombings, airplane hijackings, attacks against Washington, D.C., and other violent acts, conducted covertly by U.S. agents but with the blamed placed on Cuba. Such a plan is called a "false flag" operation and has been used by numerous countries around the world.

President John F. Kennedy canceled Operation Northwoods, rejecting the use of military force against Cuba and dismissing the chair of the Joint Chiefs. The plan was all but forgotten until the 9/11 attacks. Conspiracy theorists often cite Operation Northwoods as proof that the U.S. government would go to any lengths, even killing U.S. citizens, to achieve its political goals.

able to fly the plane into the tower, more proof that the 9/11 attacks were an inside job.

Video and photographs often can present ambiguous images that are open to interpretation by the viewer. Conspiracy theorists, without utilizing any scientific method, chose to proclaim the sinister nature of the so-called pod. At Arizona State University's Space Photography Laboratory, director Ronald Greeley has a different interpretation. After examining a high-resolution scan for *Popular Mechanics'* investigation, he concluded that the pod is nothing more than a bulge containing the plane's landing gear. Thomas Edwards, a video forensics expert, says that when digital photographs are enlarged, their resolution deteriorates into a series of squares; this process is known as pixilation. "The [online] images you view suffer from classic digital magnification. You can draw whatever conclusion you want from a bad photograph." When asked about the photos showing the pod, Edwards compares them to photographs of UFOs. "The bulge on the belly of the plane is an even harder story to swallow. You wouldn't want to go to court with this, I'll tell you that."[70]

There are other theories about the function of the pod. Some conspiracy theorists say that it contained explosives to blow up the Twin Towers. "Whoever came up with that has no idea how these things work," commented aeronautics professor Fred Culick. "You have to have the means for setting it off, releasing, and arming it. . . . It would require a lot of metalwork and wiring and, I mean, it's just harebrained. It's not like throwing an extra suitcase in the car."[71] Finally, computer simulations run by NIST demonstrated that the combination of damage to the support columns by the airplane crashes and the subsequent fires were adequate to cause the World Trade Center towers to collapse. No additional airborne explosives were necessary, and there is no evidence that such devices were used.

By the Numbers

263 MILLION

Web pages devoted to 9/11 conspiracy theories.

The Collapse of 7 World Trade Center

Even if the collapse of the Twin Towers can be proved to have been caused by speeding airliners, what caused the building known as 7 World Trade Center to fall? A forty-seven-story building located across Vesey Street just north of the towers,

7 World Trade Center was distinctive for its red masonry facade. Although it was not struck by an airplane, at 5:20 P.M. on September 11, 2001, the building collapsed, nearly seven hours after the Twin Towers fell. Video footage shows 7 World Trade Center falling straight down into its own footprint. Surely this building, say the conspiracy theorists, had to be brought down by a controlled demolition.

The SHAMRC computer simulations showed that bomb or demolition explosives would have broken more windows than those seen here in the attack.

While the conspiracy theorists simply looked at the video and then declared what they assume must have happened, NIST took the scientific approach. In its World Trade Center investigation, NIST used computer modeling to test the hypothesis of explosives causing enough structural damage to cause 7 World Trade Center to collapse. The investigators

used SHAMRC, an advanced, three-dimensional modeling program designed to analyze explosive detonations, to assess the amount of window breakage in the building as an indication of possible blast damage. The SHAMRC simulations revealed that a bomb or demolition explosives would have created many more broken windows than had actually occurred in 7 World Trade Center. In addition, if a blast had occurred, the sound would have been heard blocks away. Using another program called NLAWS, investigators determined that such a blast would have caused sound levels up to 140 decibels at 0.6 mile (1km) from the source—as loud as standing next to a jet engine. No such sound was recorded on any videos of the 7 World Trade Center collapse.

What caused the collapse of 7 World Trade Center? Computer analysis of the debris paths created as the north tower fell show that burning rubble struck 7 World Trade Center. This caused extensive damage to the exterior of the building, including the severing of seven exterior columns. Fires began on at least ten floors and continued to burn for seven hours. When the fires weakened the building's structural steel, the floors began to give way, similar to the Twin Towers. One critical interior column—column number 79—had become unsupported over nine stories due to the floor collapses and began to buckle. This led to other column failures and eventually the collapse of the entire structure. NIST's final report stated: "This was a fire-induced progressive collapse, also known as a disproportionate collapse, which is defined as the spread of local damage, from an initiating event, from element to element, eventually resulting in the collapse of an entire structure or a disproportionately large part of it."[72] Fortunately, 7 World Trade Center was evacuated, and there were no injuries or deaths in the collapse. No explosives, no conspiracy, but simply another casualty of the 9/11 terrorist attacks.

The Hole in the Pentagon

The crash of Flight 77 into the Pentagon created another wave of conspiracies in the minds of the 9/11 conspiracy theorists.

Some conspiracy theorists felt that the wingspan of a Boeing 757 like this one would have left a bigger hole in the Pentagon.

Key among these is the idea that it was not a Boeing 757 that crashed into the Pentagon, but a missile. The reasoning behind this theory is that the hole blasted into the outer wall of the Pentagon was too small to be made by a large jet airliner with a wingspan of 125 feet (38m). However, if a missile or unmanned aerial vehicle such as the military Global Hawk crashed into the Pentagon, it would make a smaller hole, such as the one created on 9/11. One conspiracy Web site presents a video clip to prove its point. According to this Web site: "You can clearly see from this video that there was never a huge gapping [sic] hole created in the Pentagon wall. The hole is only one story high, first floor and all the other floors collapsed down on top of it. There is no way a Boeing 757 could ever have gone through there."[73]

It was difficult for workers on the scene to determine the size of the entry hole due to the fires and smoke created by the crash, as well as the collapse of the damaged section of the building just twenty minutes after impact. But by examining the damage to the interior support columns, investigators from the American Society of Civil Engineers (ASCE) determined that the hole in the Pentagon's west wall measured approximately 90 (27m) feet wide. Supercomputer simulations at Purdue University confirmed the findings of the ASCE investigation. Still, a 90-foot hole is smaller than a Boeing 757's wingspan. Investigators concluded that the wings of Flight 77 were severely damaged by the impact with the Pentagon, but were also possibly damaged by striking objects on the ground

An Image of Disaster

The photograph depicts what would ordinarily be a beautiful pastoral scene: blue sky, green grass, and a bright red barn in the foreground. What transforms this picture from a charming country setting into a piece of 9/11 evidence is the huge gray cloud of smoke rising in the background. It is the aftermath of Flight 93, which crashed into a Shanksville, Pennsylvania, field just moments before the picture was taken. For Val McClatchey, the woman who took the picture, being a part of 9/11 has become a nightmare. "Any time I've done any stories," McClatchey said, "it goes online and all these conspiracy theorists start up and they call me and harass me."

McClatchey sells prints of the photograph, which she titled "The End of Serenity." Conspiracy theorists claim that McClatchey faked the photo in order to make money from the 9/11 tragedy, accusing her of using photo editing software to add the smoke cloud to her picture of an ordinary country scene. They say that the gray cloud looks more like the result of an explosives blast than the oily black smoke that would come from a plane crash. The FBI has studied the photograph and considers it authentic.

That does not stop the conspiracy theorists, who still harass McClatchey. "It's just gotten so bad, I'm just fed up with it," McClatchey said. "This thing has become too much of a distraction in my life."

Quoted in Sean D. Hamill, "Picture Made on 9/11 Takes a Toll on Photographer," New York Times, September 10, 2007. www.nytimes .com/2007/09/10/us/10cnd-shanksville.html?_r=1.

before the crash. One eyewitness reported seeing the aircraft clip several light poles as it flew toward the Pentagon. Another said that Flight 77 was so low that its right wing struck a portable power generator just before hitting the building. "Some portion of each wing was likely removed in the impacts," said ASCE probe lead investigator Paul Mlakar. "The remaining portions likely did not penetrate significantly beyond the façade."[74] Investigators thus explained the apparent discrepancy between the hole in the Pentagon and the size of the Boeing 757 that created it.

Why Conspiracies?

Why do people believe in the 9/11 conspiracies? Many people are skeptical about anything the U.S. government says. Past experiences of government officials caught telling lies and, specifically, a mistrust of the George W. Bush administration, made some people believe that their government could not be trusted to reveal the truth about 9/11. Conspiracy theories are also easy to believe in. They require no real knowledge of an event such as the 9/11 attacks. People can be led to believe in conspiracies simply by listening to others who appear to have information that they themselves lack. In addition, conspiracy theories can provide a sense of comfort in uncertain times. "Chaotic, threatening events are difficult to understand," says Phil Molé, a writer who has taken issue with the 9/11 conspiracy theories. "With [a] conspiracy theory . . . the terrible randomness of life assumes an understandable order."[75]

If people wish to believe in complicated and sinister plots supposedly surrounding 9/11, are they not free to do so? Of course, our Constitution gives anyone the right to free speech. But there is an underlying harm in believing in the 9/11 conspiracy theories. Senator John McCain explains: "Blaming some conspiracy within our government for the horrific attacks of September 11 mars the memories of all those lost on that day. . . . The 9/11 conspiracy movement exploits the public's anger and sadness." And what of the conspiracy theorists' methods? McCain says:

> They ignore the methods of science, the protocols of investigation, and the dictates of logic. The conspiracy theorists chase any bit of information, no matter how flimsy, and use it to fit their preordained conclusions. They ascribe to the government, or to some secretive group, powers wholly out of proportion to what the evidence suggests. And they ignore the facts that are present in plain sight.[76]

Science . . . investigation . . . logic. These are the hallmarks of forensic scientists, who work diligently to discover the truth in a tiny piece of debris, in a blurry video, or within the minuscule boundaries of a human cell. Knowing the truth helps us come to terms with a national tragedy such as the 9/11 attacks. And it allows us to take the necessary steps to prevent such a tragedy from ever happening again.

Notes

Introduction: A Weapon of Terror

1. Quoted in Jennifer Rosenberg, "Bombing of Pan Am Flight 103 over Lockerbie," About.com. http://history1900s.about .com/od/1980s/a/flight103.htm.

Chapter One: Terror from the Skies

2. Quoted in Mark Clayton, "Controllers' Tale of Flight 11," *Christian Science Monitor*, September 12, 2001. www.cs monitor.com/2001/0913/p1s2-usju.htm.

3. Quoted in National Commission on Terrorist Attacks, *The 9/11 Commission Report: Final Report of the National Commission on Terrorist Attacks upon the United States*. New York: Norton, 2004, p. 7.

4. Quoted in National Archives, "Staff Report, August 26, 2004," p. 10. www .archives.gov/legislative/research/9-11/ staff-report-sept2005.pdf.

5. Quoted in National Archives, "Staff Report, August 26, 2004," p. 10.

6. Quoted in National Archives, "Staff Report, August 26, 2004," p. 23.

7. Quoted in National Commission on Terrorist Attacks, *The 9/11 Commission Report*, p. 11.

8. Quoted in National Commission on Terrorist Attacks, *The 9/11 Commission Report*, pp. 6–7.

9. Quoted in National Commission on Terrorist Attacks, *The 9/11 Commission Report*, p. 8.

10. Quoted in ABC News, "ABC News Special Report: Planes Crash into World Trade Center." September 11, 2001. http:// s3.amazonaws.com/911timeline/2001/ abcnews091101.html.

11. Quoted in Alfred Goldberg, Sarandis Papadopoulos, Diane Putney, Nancy Berlage, and Rebecca Welch, *Pentagon 9/11*. Washington, DC: Historical Office, Office of the Secretary of Defense, 2007, p. 13.

12. Quoted in Goldberg et al., *Pentagon 9/11*, p. 13.

13. Quoted in Lisa Beamer with Ken Abraham, *Let's Roll!* Wheaton, IL: Tyndale House, 2002, p. 210.

14. Quoted in Beamer, *Let's Roll!* p. 212.

15. Quoted in Beamer, *Let's Roll!* p. 214.

16. Quoted in National Commission on Terrorist Attacks, *The 9/11 Commission Report*, p. 14.

17. Quoted in Dean E. Murphy, *September 11: An Oral History*. New York: Doubleday, 2002, p. 126.

18. Quoted in Robert Sullivan, ed., *One Nation: America Remembers September 11, 2001*. Boston: Little, Brown, 2001, pp. 41–42.

19. Quoted in Cathy Trost and Alicia C. Shepard, *Running Toward Danger: Stories Behind the Breaking News of 9/11*. Lanham, MD: Rowman and Littlefield, 2002, p. 84.

20. Quoted in Jim Dwyer and Kevin Flynn, *102 Minutes: The Untold Story of the Fight to Survive Inside the Twin Towers*. New York: Times, 2005, p. 223.

21. Quoted in Dwyer and Flynn, *102 Minutes*, p. 223.

Chapter Two: The Search at Ground Zero

22. Quoted in Chris Bull and Sam Erman, eds., *At Ground Zero: 25 Stories from Young Reporters Who Were There*. New York: Thunder's Mouth, 2002, p. 100.

23. Quoted in Shiya Ribowsky and Tom Shachtman, *Dead Center: Behind the Scenes at the World's Largest Medical Examiner's Office*. New York: Regan, 2006, p. 169.

24. Ribowsky and Shachtman, *Dead Center*, p. 157.

25. Quoted in Bradley J. Adams and John E. Byrd, eds., *Recovery, Analysis, and Identification of Commingled Human Remains*. Totowa, NJ: Humana, 2008, p. 133.

26. Quoted in Adams and Byrd, *Recovery, Analysis, and Identification of Commingled Human Remains*, p. 135.

27. Robert C. Shaler, *Who They Were: Inside the World Trade Center DNA Story: The Unprecedented Effort to Identify the Missing*. New York: Free Press, 2005, pp. 33–34.

28. Shaler, *Who They Were*, p. 36.

29. Ribowsky and Shachtman, *Dead Center*, p. 158.

30. Quoted in Goldberg, et al., *Pentagon 9/11*, p. 180.

31. Quoted in Peter Perl, "Hallowed Ground," *Washington Post*, May 12, 2002. www.washingtonpost.com/ac2/wp-dyn?pagename=article&node=&contentId=A56110-2002May8.

32. Quoted in Shaler, *Who They Were*, p. 321.

Chapter Three: Identifying the Terrorists

33. Kenneth J. Williams, memo to FBI Counterterrorism Unit, U.S. Department of Justice, July 10, 2001. www.usdoj.gov/oig/special/0506/app2.htm.

34. Quoted in Peter Finn, "Hamburg's Cauldron of Terror," *Washington Post*, September 11, 2002. www.washingtonpost.com/wp-dyn/articles/A64793-2002Sep10.html.

35. Quoted in Cryptome, *The United States of America vs. Zacarias Moussaoui*, trial transcript. http://cryptome.org/usa-v-zm-030706-02.htm.

36. Quoted in U.S. Senate Select Committee on Intelligence and U.S. House Permanent

Select Committee on Intelligence, *Joint Inquiry into Intelligence Community Activities Before and After the Terrorist Attacks of September 11, 2001*, GPO Access, December 2002, p. 135. www.gpoaccess.gov/serialset/creports/911.html.

37. Quoted in U.S. Senate Select Committee on Intelligence and U.S. House Permanent Select Committee on Intelligence, *Joint Inquiry into Intelligence Community Activities Before and After the Terrorist Attacks of September 11, 2001*, p. 138.

38. Quoted in U.S. Senate Select Committee on Intelligence and U.S. House Permanent Select Committee on Intelligence, *Joint Inquiry into Intelligence Community Activities Before and After the Terrorist Attacks of September 11, 2001*, p. 139.

39. Quoted in CNN, "Hijackers Conducted Surveillance Flights Ahead of 9/11." http://archives.cnn.com/2002/US/09/27/hijackers/index.html.

40. Quoted in U.S. House of Representatives, *The Congressional Record*, GPO Access, June 27, 2005. www.gpoaccess.gov/crecord.

41. Quoted in Josh White, "Hijackers Were Not Identified Before 9/11, Investigation Says," *Washington Post*, September 22, 2006. www.washingtonpost.com/wp-dyn/content/article/2006/09/21/AR2006092101831.html.

42. Shaler, *Who They Were*, p. 299.

43. Quoted in Eve Conant, "Remains of the Day," *Newsweek*, January 12, 2009, p. 45.

44. Quoted in *Frontline*, "Inside the Terror Network," PBS. www.pbs.org/wgbh/pages/frontline/shows/network/personal/instructions.html.

45. Quoted in Conant, "Remains of the Day," p. 44.

46. Quoted in Conant, "Remains of the Day," p. 43.

47. Quoted in Conant, "Remains of the Day," p. 44.

48. Quoted in Conant, "Remains of the Day," p. 43.

Chapter Four: Why the Towers Fell

49. Quoted in James Glanz and Eric Lipton, *City in the Sky: The Rise and Fall of the World Trade Center*. New York: Times, 2003, p. 107.

50. Quoted in Angus Kress Gillespie, *Twin Towers: The Life of New York City's World Trade Center*. New Brunswick, NJ: Rutgers University Press, 1999, p. 81.

51. Quoted in Glanz and Lipton, *City in the Sky*, p. 131.

52. Quoted in Eric Nalder, "Twin Towers Engineered to Withstand Jet Collision," *Seattle Times*, February 27, 1993. http://community.seattletimes.nwsource.com/archive/?date=19930227&slug=1687698.

53. Quoted in China.org.cn, "Baosteel Will Recycle World Trade Center Debris," January 24, 2002. www.china.org.cn/english/2002/Jan/25776.htm.

54. Quoted in Kenneth Chang, "Scarred Steel Holds Clues, and Remedies," *New York Times*, October 2, 2001. http://www.nytimes.com/2001/10/02/science/scarred-steel-holds-clues-and-remedies.html.

55. Quoted in James Glanz and Kenneth Chang, "A Nation Challenged: The Site; Engineers Seek to Test Steel Before It Is Melted for Reuse," *New York Times*, September 29, 2001. http://www.nytimes.com/2001/09/29/nyregion/nation-challenged-site-engineers-seek-test-steel-before-it-melted-for-reuse.html.

56. Quoted in *NOVA*, "Why the Towers Fell," PBS, April 30, 2002. www.pbs.org/wgbh/nova/transcripts/2907_wtc.html.

57. Quoted in *NOVA*, "Why the Towers Fell."

58. Quoted in Noah Shachtman, "Tower Wreckage Reveals Clues," *Wired*, October 5, 2001. www.wired.com/politics/law/news/2001/10/47357.

59. Quoted in American Society of Civil Engineers, *Testimony of Dr. W. Gene Corley on Behalf of the American Society of Civil Engineers, Before the Subcommittee on Environment, Technology and Standards, & Subcommittee on Research, Committee on Science, U.S. House of Representatives*, March 6, 2002, p. 6. www.asce.org/pdf/3-6-02wtc_testimony.pdf.

60. Quoted in *NOVA*, "Why the Towers Fell."

Chapter Five: Conspiracy?

61. Richard Roeper, *Debunked! Conspiracy Theories, Urban Legends, and Evil Plots of the 21st Century*. Chicago: Chicago Review, 2008, p. 5.

62. Jerry Russell, "Proof of Controlled Demolition at the WTC," Attack OnAmerica.net. www.attackonamerica.net/proofofcontrolleddemolitionatwtc.htm.

63. National Institute of Standards and Technology, *Final Report on the Collapse of the World Trade Center Towers*. Technology Administration, U.S. Department of Commerce, September 2005, p. 29. National Institute of Standards and Technology World Trade Center Web Site. http://wtc.nist.gov/NCSTAR1/NCSTAR1index.htm.

64. Quoted in Allison Gilbert, Phil Hirschkorn, Melinda Murphy, Robyn Walensky, and Mitchell Stephens, eds., *Covering Catastrophe: Broadcast Journalists Report September 11*. Chicago: Bonus Books, 2002, p. 78.

65. Quoted in ABC News, "ABC News Special Report."

66. Quoted in *NOVA*, "Why the Towers Fell."

67. Quoted in David Dunbar and Brad Reagan, eds., *Debunking 9/11 Myths: Why Conspiracy Theories Can't Stand Up to the Facts*. New York: Hearst, 2006, p. 45.

68. Quoted in Dunbar and Reagan, *Debunking 9/11 Myths*, p. 46.

69. 9-11 Review, "Alleged Hijackers." http://911review.com/myth/hijackers.html.

70. Quoted in Dunbar and Reagan, *Debunking 9/11 Myths*, pp. 10–11.

71. Quoted in Dunbar and Reagan, *Debunking 9/11 Myths*, p. 11.

72. National Institute of Standards and Technology, *Final Report on the Collapse of World Trade Center Building 7*. Technology Administration, U.S. Department of Commerce, August, 2008, p. xxxii. National Institute of Standards and Technology World Trade Center Web Site. http://wtc.nist.gov/NCSTAR1/NCSTAR1index.htm.

73. Freedom Files Website, "Flight 77 and the Pentagon Crash—What Really Happened Here?" www.freedomfiles.org/war/pentagon.htm.

74. Quoted in Dunbar and Reagan, *Debunking 9/11 Myths*, p. 68.

75. Phil Molé, "9/11 Conspiracy Theories: The 9/11 Truth Movement in Perspective," *eSkeptic*, September 11, 2006. www.skeptic.com/eskeptic/06-09-11.html.

76. Quoted in Dunbar and Reagan, *Debunking 9/11 Myths*, pp. xiv–xv.

For More Information

Books

David Dunbar and Brad Reagan, eds., *Debunking 9/11 Myths: Why Conspiracy Theories Can't Stand Up to the Facts*. New York: Hearst, 2006. This book takes on many of the conspiracy theorists' favorite theories about 9/11 and presents logical, although more ordinary, alternative explanations.

Mitch Frank, *Understanding September 11: Answering Questions About the Attacks on America*. New York: Viking, 2002. Presents basic information about 9/11 in an easy-to-understand question-and-answer format. Includes black-and-white photographs and maps.

Mark P. Friedlander Jr. and Terry M. Phillips, *When Objects Talk: Solving a Crime with Science*. Minneapolis, MN: Lerner, 2001. Forensic science is examined in this book, with chapters highlighting the various methods forensic investigators use to solve crimes.

Sid Jacobson and Ernie Colón, *The 9/11 Report: A Graphic Adaptation*. New York: Hill and Wang, 2006. This is a condensed version of the official report of the 9/11 Commission in a full-color, graphic novel–style adaptation. Includes a foldout time line of the four 9/11 hijackings.

Tamara L. Roleff, *The World Trade Center Attack*. San Diego, CA: Greenhaven, 2003. A look at the 9/11 attacks and their aftermath in the words of those who were personally affected by them. Included are personal accounts from survivors and rescue workers, as well as political figures such as President George W. Bush and Osama bin Laden.

Gail B. Stewart, *Forensics*. Detroit: Lucent, 2006. A detailed examination of the role of forensics in criminal investigation. Includes numerous black-and-white photographs, plus maps and charts.

DVD

NOVA. "Why the Towers Fell." PBS, 2002. A fascinating look at the efforts of experts to determine why the Twin Towers collapsed on September 11, 2001. Includes interviews with forensic engineers, including the man who designed the towers' structure, and computer simulations of the airliner crashes.

Internet Source

Anthony Bruno, "The World Trade Center Story: The Port Authority Police Department," TruTV.com. www.trutv .com/library/crime/terrorists_spies/ terrorists/papd/1.html.

Web Sites

911 Truth (www.911truth.org). One of the primary sites for presenting theories that question the official 9/11 Commission's findings and promoting the idea that a government conspiracy was behind the 9/11 attacks.

Department of Homeland Security (www.dhs.gov). The official Web site of the department charged with protecting America against terrorist attacks and natural disasters.

DNA Initiative (www.dna.gov/basics). Presents a thorough explanation of the use of DNA in forensic investigation. Provides numerous links for more information.

Federal Bureau of Investigation Counterterrorism Web Page (www.fbi.gov/terrorinfo/counterrorism/waronterrorhome.htm). Discusses the FBI's efforts to prevent terrorism at home and to help dismantle terror networks around the world.

Flight 93 National Memorial Web Site (www.honorflight93.org). A Web site to honor the heroes of Flight 93.

Forensics for Kids, All About Forensic Science (www.all-about-forensic-science.com/science-for-kids.html). Contains links to various Web sites that will help students understand forensics.

Index

Picture Credits

About the Author

Craig E. Blohm has written numerous magazine articles on historical subjects for children for more than twenty years and has authored many books for Lucent Books. A native of Chicago, he has written for social studies textbooks and conducted workshops in writing history for children.